THE STORY OF THOMAS MORE

THOMAS MORE

The Story of
THOMAS MORE

by JOHN FARROW

Sheed and Ward • New York • 1954

NIHIL OBSTAT
PATRICK J. DIGNAN
Censor Librorum

IMPRIMATUR
✠JAMES FRANCIS CARDINAL MCINTYRE
Archbishop of Los Angeles

Los Angeles
July 21, 1954

Hoc opusculum
Eduardo J. Whelan
amico, sacerdoti, ac
sodali Ignatiano apprime vero
dicatum.

FOREWORD

THE reader will soon discover that my aim was not to write an exhaustive biography in the conventional sense, but to tell a story in general terms of a man and his friends and his enemies; his time and circumstance; a story of tenderness and violence and tragedy, and, above all, a story of courage and example. I am indebted to Fr. Joseph Donovan, S.J., Dean of Law at Loyola University in Los Angeles, who encouraged me to write the book and who, at the planning stage, took me to the Huntington Library. There, thanks to the graciousness of the Library officials, my appetite was stimulated by the famous Holbein collection and the treasure of papers and books of the period. The Assistant to the Librarian, Miss Gertrude Ruhnka, consented to aid me in the compilation of the considerable research. This she did most ably and I thank her deeply. Upon completion of the writing, I sent the manuscript to a More scholar and fellow devotee then in London, Dr. Frank Sullivan. He interrupted his busy literary labours at the British Museum to make valuable suggestions and criticism. I thank him also.

J. F.

THE STORY OF THOMAS MORE

I

IT was because of a scruple that he chose death and it would have been easy for him, skilled in the law as he was, to divert that scruple with the twist of argument or the placation of compromise. But he followed the way of his conscience and accepted a tyrant's revenge. Death was then the frequent punishment, delivered in all manner of device. The swift down-glitter of the headsman's axe, the hot pincers, the hack and chop of the quartering process, the stake, the rack, the gibbet, were all part of a pattern which provided no exemption when the King's anger was provoked. The sight of men being put to death was ordinary enough in the year 1535, yet, when the head of Thomas More was set high on London Bridge, England was shocked, and indignation swept Christendom. "I would rather," declared the Emperor Charles V, "have lost the best city in my dominion than such a counsellor as More."

He was fifty-seven when he climbed the scaffold, respected for goodness and wisdom, learning and wit. He was a statesman and a patriot, but high office had never been permitted to usurp the duties of a parent. He was the friend of Erasmus, and he had been the confidant of the prince who sent him to his death. He had written *Utopia*, and he had been Lord Chancellor of England, but in all manner of circumstance his conduct was characterized by a humility and calmness of spirit which did not desert him at the end. He was then calm enough to jest with his executioner, humble enough to invite the prayers of the crowd. Splendid and triumphant was his final utterance, that he died "the King's good servant, but God's first."

He had the vision of a great reformer and he possessed the genius to translate his hopes and dreams into an understandable form and pattern. He yearned for a better world for all men. And he was one of the first victims of a Revolution which was unique in that it was for the privileged and engineered by the privileged.

He was truly one of the great Christians, and the lustre of his virtues and his talents has survived and grown with the centuries. The acid-tongued Dean Swift described him as "the person of the greatest virtue this kingdom ever produced." Four hundred years after his death Pope Pius XI proclaimed that his name had been added to the roll of the Saints. The cathedrals of the world celebrated.

Not only at the altars was he paid tribute. More was coming into his own as a major prophet of social progress, and even in Russia his *Utopia* was being studied and admired, although misunderstood. In Moscow an institution bearing the name of Karl Marx communicates with an

English convent, seeking information on what is a mutual interest, his life and work and death.

"Nothing speaks more eloquently for the greatness of the man," wrote the socialist Karl Kautsky, "nothing shows more distinctly how he towered above his contemporaries, than that it required more than three centuries before the conditions existed which enable us to perceive he set himself aims which are not the idle dreaming of a leisure hour, but the result of a profound insight into the essentials of the economic tendencies of his age. Although *Utopia* is more than four hundred years old, the ideals of More are not vanquished but still lie before a striving mankind.'"

2

THOMAS MORE was born on the sixth of February, 1478, the year following the publication of the first printed book in England. While not of noble rank, the families of his parents were of consequence. His father, John More, was a prosperous barrister, afterwards made a Knight and Judge of the King's Bench. His maternal grandfather, after whom he was named, also achieved distinction in the same profession and was, in 1503, elected Sheriff of London.

In the colourful story of England there seldom has been a more vivid period. The passing of the fifteenth century and the coming of the sixteenth presented a pageant which was reflected in the turbulent streets of London itself. The rich dress of the merchants and aldermen, scarlet and blue, velvet and gold, their feasts and their arguments, their processions and celebrations, the great banquets and public executions, the King and his Court, the nobles and their retinues, the brawling and jostling, the hawking and vending, the humour and violence, the great solemnities of the Church, the almost continual tolling of deep- and sweet-toned bells, all these made for a scene which prompted the poet Dunbar to sing:

London, thou art of Townes A per se
Soveraign of cities, semeliest in sight
Of high renoun, riches and royaltie;
Of Lordis, Barons, and many goodly Knyght;
Of most delectable lusty ladies bright;
Of famous Prelatis, in habitis clericall;
Of Merchauntis full of substance and myght:
London, thou art the flour of Cities all.[1]

John More, the father of Thomas More, fitted well his place and time. He liked life and lived fully, a man of vigour and shrewdness and wit. Commenting on the hazards of matrimony, it was he who compared the multitude of women who were to be chosen for wives to "a bag full of snakes and eels together, seven snakes for one eel."[2] The good Judge had his laugh, but he was not daunted by the odds. Four times he went to the altar, taking his last bride near his seventieth birthday. He had six children, Joan, Thomas, Agatha, John, Edward, and Elizabeth. Thomas was the second child, junior by three years to his sister Joan. Their mother's name was Agnes, and she called her first son after her father, Thomas Granger.

Lawyer More sent his son to St. Anthony's school on Threadneedle Street, then the best in London and possessed of an ancient reputation. Medievalism was on the wane. The printing press was a fact. Scholastic methods in England were about to feel the impact of an intellectual revolution which was already flourishing south of the Alps. But it is doubtful if any changes had yet arrived to disturb the old ways at St. Anthony's. Books were scarce. Discipline was severe. The pupils were trained by memory and disputation. Latin was the main subject. The headmaster was Nicholas Holt, an energetic man who took a liking to young Thomas More and recognized his worth. The boy was assiduous and cheerful and became a leader among his fellows.

Holt was a friend of John Morton, Archbishop of Canterbury and Lord Chancellor of the realm. Access to such a powerful figure was valuable, and shrewd John More was not a man to neglect opportunity. It was the custom for the nobility and the gentle-born to school their sons by putting them into the houses of the great. As a respected barrister John More exerted considerable influence in the City and this influence, along with the headmaster's recommendation, sufficed to have Thomas appointed page to the prelate.

He was about twelve years old when he went to live at Lambeth Palace, a dazzling experience for a bright and observant lad. Here, in the shadow of the archiepiscopal chair, he witnessed a continuous flow of politicians and petitioners, envoys and churchmen. He was attendant at the great functions, playing his role in the complicated etiquette of the time. On more private occasions he would be there too, standing behind his master, ready to pass the goblet or run the errand, always watching, listening, learning.

Archbishop Morton was an astute statesman who had successfully weathered the vicissitudes of civil war, exile, and imprisonment, and who was now adviser to the King, Henry VII. In 1493 he was made a Cardinal. More was to describe him (in *Utopia*) as "a man . . . not more honourable for his authority, than for his prudence and virtue. He was of a mean stature, and though stricken in age, yet bare he his body upright. In his face did shine such an amiable reverence, as was pleasant to behold, gentle in communication, yet earnest and sage. He had great delight many times with rough speech to his suitors to prove, but without harm, what prompt wit, and what bold spirit were in every man. In the which as in a virtue much agreeing with his nature, so that therewith were not joined impudence, he took great delectation. And the same person, as apt and mete to have an administration in the weal publique, he did lovingly embrace. In his speech, he was fine, eloquent and pithy. In the law he had profound knowledge, in wit he was incomparable, and in memory wonderful excellent. These qualities, which in him were by nature singular, he by learning and use had made perfect. The King put much trust in his counsel, the weal publique also in a manner leaned unto him, when I was there. For even in the chief of his youth, he was taken from school into the Court, and there passed all his time in much trouble and business, being continually tumbled and tossed in the ways of diverse misfortunes and adversities. And so by many and great dangers he learned the experience of the world, which being so learned can not easily be forgotten . . ." [3]

The cheerful face, the winning nature of his page did not escape the attention or affection of the old man. Oftentimes, to amuse his guests, the Archbishop would have plays performed by professional players. It became a feature on these occasions for young Thomas to step in amongst the actors, creating his own part and speeches as the play went along. This he did with great skill and to much applause. "This child here waiting at the table," said his patron, "whosoever shall live to see it, will prove a marvellous man." [4]

The dexterity and magnitude of Morton's political abilities, particularly in controlling the power of the great feudal landowners, have often been compared to the accomplishment of Cardinal Richelieu. Proximity to such a mentor could not fail to have its effect upon the boy's mind. When writing his *Life of Richard III* he gave a typical example of the Cardinal's discreet wisdom. As the Usurper, Richard had sent the Duke of Buckingham to discover whether Morton was for or against him. "In good faith, my Lord," was the reply, "I love not much to talk much of Princes as a thing not all out of peril, though the word be without fault, forasmuch as it shall not be taken as the party meant it, but as it pleaseth the Prince to construe it." [5]

In the second year of young More's attendance upon the Archbishop there was a great rejoicing at Lambeth Castle. A second son was born to Henry VII and it was announced that the babe would carry the name of his father. The dynasty was strengthened and the streets of London were made ready for festivity. The Lord Chancellor gave a banquet at his residence. Prayers were said, speeches made, wine poured. It was an exciting time for the young page. This was in the summer of 1491. Across the seas, in far away Granada, a sober-faced little princess was giving thanks to God that her father was driving the Moors from Spain. She was Catalina, better known as Catherine of Aragon. Elaborate messages of congratulations went from her parents to England, for they had the fullest expectations that their daughter would marry Arthur, the King's first son.

Among those of the English nobility who did not participate heartily in the royal festivities was Thomas Howard, Earl of Surrey and later second Duke of Norfolk. This nobleman did not come to London but remained in the dark halls of his castle, gloomily watching his favourite daughter, Elizabeth, still with her dolls. Marriage prospects for her were not too bright. Her father had many children and had been in disrepute at Court, although he was now pardoned and soon to be made Lieutenant of the North. In his veins flowed Plantagenet blood, but he was content, when she arrived at the proper age, to wed Elizabeth to a knight.

His son-in-law was no ordinary knight. While it was true that his paternal grandfather was a London wool merchant, his mother was noble-born. He was also very rich, an important factor in the reasoning of any parent. Lastly, he was ambitious. He was Sir Thomas Boleyn, and his third child by Elizabeth was a daughter called Anne. But this birth, so important in our story, was not to be for fifteen years or so. The future Henry VIII had just been born, Thomas More was yet a boy in the service of Morton, and at Oxford University young Thomas Wolsey, son of an Ipswich butcher, enjoyed his first grasp at fame. But the actors were being assembled, the stage was being set, the drama was almost to begin, the drama which was to bring Thomas More great tragedy but a greater glory.

Valuable environment though Lambeth Palace was for his page, the Archbishop realized that too long a stay among the many activities of his household might twist a boy's charm and cleverness into a disagreeable precocity. After two years he made arrangements for the next step in his protégé's education and the boy was sent to Canterbury College at Oxford.

It was the same year that Columbus made his landfall, and the University was experiencing the commencement of a dispute born of the Italian Renaissance but having a bent of its own. The new interest in the Greek tongue, inspired by William Selling and the Italian Vitelli, had split the University into two portions, the Greeks and the Trojans. More, upon his arrival, appears to have allied himself with the Greeks. He was fortunate in having for his Greek professor, the learned William Grocyn, who, upon his return from Italy some six years before, had begun the teaching of Greek at Oxford. More also derived instruction in Greek from Thomas Linacre, who, like Grocyn, had studied in Italy. But the outstanding figure among the Renaissance scholars in England at this period was Grocyn's illustrious pupil, John Colet, later to become More's confessor.

Inspired by the spirit of Humanism these men fought an impassioned battle against medieval reactionism. They became known as the Oxford Reformers but, unlike the Protestant reformers who came after them, they sought no schism with Rome. Rather than bring innovation to dogma, they worked to eradicate ecclesiastical abuses and to widen the horizons of learning. They gathered disciples and read the New Testament in the Greek text. They raised their voices against the worldliness of the clergy and the sale of bishoprics. They quoted the Pauline Epistles. They studied Aristotle and Quintilian and Seneca. They applauded Plato's ideal community. They dreamed of a practical application of Christian principles, of giving life to theories. While scanning the past, they hoped for the future. Feudalism with its favours for few and serfdom for many was dying. The capitalistic state, bringing no betterment for the majority, was about to be born. In the stormy transition between the two systems, these few scholars of Oxford fought valiantly to direct their philosophy and faith into action. To better the lot of all men was both their science and their passion, it was the creed which inspired Thomas More to write his *Utopia*.

Another supporter of the revival of letters then at the University was Thomas Wolsey, whose brilliance had won him his Bachelor's degree before he was sixteen and who soon was to be made a Fellow of Magdalen and finally Senior Bursar of the College. He was only six years older than More, and the two must have known each other, but there is no record of any meeting or friendship. When More was resident at Canterbury College, Wolsey was already something of a figure in the University, but More was not of a mould to court his senior. Wolsey, on his part, never allowed the fervour of the "New Learning" to thaw the cold ambition which directed his every step. The son of a London lawyer could have been of little interest to one who eagerly pursued patronage and who eventually found a benevolent patron in the person of the Marquis of Dorset.

Wolsey and More were unalike in many ways as men can be, in others they were curiously similar. Both were remarkable scholars, masters of rhetoric and logic, engaging in presence and conversation, standing well out from their fellows. Destiny was to brush their lives together in a strange manner. One, in scarlet magnificence, was to live with a splendour never seen before or since in England. The other, in hair shirt, singing in a parish choir, was to be criticized because of the modesty of his ways. One was to succeed the other as Lord Chancellor of England. Both were to win the fickle esteem of Henry VIII and both were to attract the petulant anger of young Anne Boleyn. "I die the King's good servant, but God's first," said More as he faced martyrdom. "If I had served God as diligently as I have done the King," wept Wolsey from the depths of ignominy, "He would not have given me over in my gray hairs."

Life at Oxford at the close of the fifteenth century was harsh and regulated by monastic discipline. The day began with Mass at five, studies commenced at six. The hours of prayer and study were long, and violations of either met with prompt severity. Latin, except at the time of the principal festivals, was the language of the Halls and a student was fined when he broke the rule. Older students were expected to coach their juniors, and in the morning the Bachelors and Masters gave lectures. The first meal was not served until ten in the morning, the second and last at five in the afternoon. The food was meager. The afternoons were usually devoted to examination, discussion, and disputation. The student had to attend all Church ceremonies, and every member of a Hall was required to be in by eight in the evening. More suffered all the hardships of a poor scholar, for his father gave him a very scant allowance. But he bore his father no ill will and later wrote: "Thus it came to pass that I indulged in no vice or vain pleasure, that I did not spend my time in dangerous or idle pastimes, that I did not even know the meaning of extravagance and luxury, that I did not learn to put money to evil uses, that, in fine, I had no love, or even thought, of anything beyond my studies." [6]

Poverty did not prevent More from being happy at Oxford. There was much to compensate for the rigours. The beauty of the buildings and landscape, the comfort of intellectual comradeship, the joy of study, fitted his nature. Nor did he find ecclesiastical rule too irksome. He was never, as successful lawyer or high official, to abandon the habit and exercise of ordered prayer. There was always a great deal of the priest in him. In those crowded days at the University he must have pondered over his fitness to hold the Chalice and prepare the Sacrifice. His friends and teachers, indeed most of the undergraduates at that time, were in Holy Orders. The Church was the sure highway to success and security for the brilliant, yet More chose another road. But to his death the monastic life held a fascination for him. When, during his imprisonment in the Tower, his daughter Margaret wept at the sight of his cell he told her: "I assure thee on my faith, my own good daughter, if it had not been for my wife and you that be my children, whom I account the chief part of my charge, I would not have failed long ere this to have closed myself in as strait a room, and straiter too." [7]

He had been at Oxford less than two years when John

More became alarmed at the direction of his son's education. The London lawyer had little interest in the dispute over the Greek revival, nor did he wish his son to adopt a contemplative life. He wanted his son to follow his own footsteps and wear the long robe of the Law, the best and most sensible, in his opinion, of secular pursuits. He abruptly took the youth from the University and brought him to London.

It was a wrench for the young student to leave Oxford and all that it meant. He offered no rebellion to the parental will, but he did not permit departure from the University to end the interests and friendships which had been nurtured there. His absorption in the Greek revival remained unabated, and it was in London that he achieved full participation in the movement. The hours of his apprenticeship in Law were long, but somehow he found time to continue the learning which he had begun at Canterbury College. Under the watchful eyes of his father he was initiated into the mysteries of writs and procedure at New Inn, an Inn of Chancery. He had little taste for the family profession; nevertheless he accepted his destiny with docility and good heart.

The teaching of Canon Law and Civil Law was the property of the great Universities, but the Inns of Court in London and their affiliated Inns of Chancery produced the actual practitioners of English Common Law. The four Inns of Court, Lincoln's, Gray's, the Inner Temple, and the Middle Temple, along with the Inns of Chancery, where a young man was introduced to ethics, politics, and the foundations of jurisprudence, comprised what in fact was a legal university. The student was instructed in history,

scripture, music, "dancing and other nobleman's pastimes."
But Law was the ruling subject, taught by lecture, argument,
and rehearsal of procedure. Each Inn was a highly organ-
ized society with complicated government by many officers
of various grades and seniority. The council consisting of
masters of the bench was the top of the hierarchy, then came
the utter-barristers, those already admitted to the law.
There were four elected governors, the Autumn and Lent
readers, the dean of the Chapel, the keeper of the Black
Books, the marshall, the pensioner, the butler for Christmas,
the steward for Christmas, the master of the revels, the chief
butler, and the chaplain. Ceremonies and revels gave colour
to a routine which, although disciplined, was nothing like
as strict as More had experienced at Oxford. His fellow
students in London seem to have been singularly high-
spirited, for the records of the time show that Francis Sutt-
well, John Pole, and Henry Smyth "were put out of the
commons for playing at dice." [8] Another rowdy character
was fined three shillings and fourpence for breaking into a
tavern and beating the wife of the proprietor. Still another
was similarly penalized for assaulting the wife of the Inn's
gardener. The butler was attacked by one of the students
with drawn sword, and so the roll goes on, a litany of tur-
bulence and rule breaking.

The same diligence, the same rapid facility he had shown
in the past, accompanied More's application to law. After
the required stay at New Inn he moved on to the wider
opportunities of Lincoln's Inn. There he rapidly won attention and reward and was promoted Reader of Furnival's
Inn, an affiliate of Lincoln's. The position of Reader in the
Inns was similar to that of a professor in a university. More

gave lectures and supervised the activity of students. He had both the esteem of his superiors and the respect of his juniors, and it is surprising, in view of his quick prominence, that he did not incur the dislike of the less favoured. But he had a natural charm, and his industry was leavened by a wit which saved him from the gloom of pedantry. He played his part in the revels and merry games of the Inns, and his popularity was endorsed by a large attendance at his lectures. Long before his apprenticeship was concluded he excelled in the many devices of the barrister's trade. He was persuasive of speech, quick with question, ready with answer, master of logic and procedure. His reputation exceeded his years and spread beyond the precincts of the Inns. A brilliant career seemed certain for him when he was finally called to the Bar, but he was not prompt to plead in the Courts. Religion and literature were still his fondest interests. He had obeyed his father and learned the Law, but doubt still haunted him.

Exercise in the Greek tongue and in philosophy had kept pace with More's acquisition of legal knowledge. The hours spent in study while he was an inmate of the Inns were formidable, made possible only because of an exceptional ability and extreme self-discipline. He slept not more than four or five hours, and for a bed he used a plank with a log for a pillow. One of his extraordinary talents was the power to absorb the meaning of sentences as a whole, at a single glance. "Everybody who has ever existed," wrote a friend, "has had to put his sentences together from words, except our Thomas More alone. He, on the contrary, possesses the super-grammatical art, and particularly in reading Greek." [9]

Some of his Oxford friends had come to London, and their shared interest in the Greek revival insured more continuing enthusiasm in the joys of learning. John Grocyn, his tutor at the University, was now vicar in the church of St. Lawrence Jewry. Thomas Linacre was busy with the foundation of the society which became the Royal College of Physicians. John Colet was canon of St. Martin le Grand, soon to be appointed Dean of St. Paul's and after to establish his famous school of that name, marking a new system of education. William Lily, the Greek scholar, was to become first headmaster of St. Paul's. Colet was More's confessor, and when he was absent from London, More wrote to him: "Meantime, I pass my time with Grocyn, who is, as you know, in your absence the guide of my life, with Linacre the guide of my studies, and with our friend Lily, my dearest friend." [10]

The enthusiasts indulged in a constant and pleasant competition. They wrote verse and epigrams. They translated Greek into Latin and Latin into English. More participated fully in these friendly rivalries. He also wrote playlets for the revels at the Inns, and somehow he found time to collaborate with Lily on a Latin translation of epigrams from Greek anthology.

3

JUDGE MORE resented the literary activities of his son that seemed so far removed from the practical studies and conventional pastimes of the Inns. He was a man of common sense, who had arranged and set the goal of a safe and prosperous living for his son. He was proud of Thomas' progress in the Inns, but he could not understand these other diversions. He considered them to be a waste of time, dangerous to his plan. An argument arose between father and son, and in an attempt to uphold parental authority, the Judge reduced Thomas's allowance to a pittance.

John More was not wrong in thinking that his plans for his son's career were in danger. The altar still beckoned to Thomas, even though he worried over his fitness to approach it. There was little doubt where his heart lay, and his appearance in the pulpit of St. Lawrence's Church, where he lectured on St. Augustine's City of God, created a minor sensation. His friend Grocyn, Vicar of the church, persuaded him to this action, and the applause of a distinguished audience made it a spectacular triumph for the young layman.

A second great influence in More's life at this time was provided by the holy men of the Carthusian Order, still in possession of their celebrated London Charterhouse. Here, in buildings founded by an illustrious Crusader, the white-clad monks led a solitary and contemplative existence, regulated by lengthy devotions, studies, and hard manual labour. Stout adherence to stern rule was then, as now, characteristic of an Order which in its long history has never experienced the need for reform. To those austere men, More brought his perplexities, asking them to assist in the scrutiny of his conscience. Should he take the vows and wear the cowl of their Order? Should he be simple priest or Franciscan friar? Or was it his destiny that he should remain a layman? They gave a wise decision. Thomas More was to come and live with the monks, but he was not to take vows. Time and prayer and contemplation would furnish the answer to his problems, but until he was sure of that answer, he was not to sever relations with temporal responsibilities.

More went to the Charterhouse with high purpose and strong resolve and, as far as his studies would permit, he steadfastly lived as an ordinary monk. He was given a pallet in a solitary cell and he wore a hair shirt to "tame his flesh." He observed the rules of silence and of fasting, for the monks ate but twice a day and then sparingly and without meat. He rose early in the morning to attend long devotions. There were fixed hours of prayer all through the day, and near midnight he left his cell again to assist in the singing of Matins and Lauds of the Dead. Every night and in darkness, save for the flicker of the sanctuary light and a few oil lamps, the monks chanted for nearly three hours. It was an impressive, but surely a melancholy, exercise, for the monks sang with a dolorous note. "As the duty of a good monk is rather to lament than to sing," say the rubrics, "we must so sing that lamentation, not the joy of singing, be in our hearts."

For nearly three years Thomas More remained with the Carthusian Order, then of a sudden he left the Charterhouse and wholeheartedly gave his attention to public affairs and the practice of Law. The sixteenth century was but three years old when this quick departure from the cloister occurred, and the two years following saw More established as a barrister, elected to Parliament, and married to a country miss from Essex.

What occasioned this abrupt change of thought and action? The question of priest, monk, or layman had been solved in favour of the last, but certainly not because of loss of faith. More remained deeply religious, even to the degree of continuing to subject himself to the penance of the hair shirt. The decision could not have been born of mere whim or impulse. The period of self-examination had been too long, his nature too prudent.

According to family tradition recorded by his great-grandson, Cresacre More, he proposed to pattern his life after a singular layman, Pico della Mirandola, whose biography had been written by his nephew. More translated the book and studied it diligently. There was much in the Italian's nature and circumstance akin to his own, although there were many things dissimilar. Both had been endowed with high intellect and personal charm and good fortune. Both were fascinated by philosophy and theology. Both saw the need for clerical reform. Both had felt the urge of religious life, the haunting feeling that a rejection of it would be wrong, the knowledge that the taking of so solemn a step, and finding oneself unfit, would be worse. The Italian had finally resolved to wear the Dominican habit but died before taking his vows.

Medievalism brought rogues, as well as saints, to take the tonsure, and More must have known many in the clerical state who took their vows lightly. In a structure where secular positions and powers were often held by men in orders there was not the same opprobrium attached to the worldly priest as there is now. In Thomas More the disavowal of a vocation was, in a sense, proof of his piety. For such as he, already known as scholar and orator, the Church was a sure road to preferment and power had he been a creature of ambition. Thomas Wolsey, on leaving Oxford, had served as one of the chaplains to the Archbishop of Canterbury and was now holding a similar appointment to Sir Richard Nanfan, Deputy-Governor of Calais. For the true ascetic, and this More was, it was sacrifice to leave the tranquillity of the cloister, to reject the mysteries of contemplative life. The question persists. Why did he so suddenly and so ardently become the busy lawyer, the fervent husband? Was the long self-examination a deliberate test to determine his allegiance to chastity, an effort to ascertain whether he was better suited to receive the Sacrament of Matrimony rather than the Sacrament of Orders?

A bishop warns the aspirant to the subdiaconate: "You ought anxiously to consider again and again what sort of a burden this is which you are taking upon you of your own accord. Up to this you are free. You may still, if you choose, turn to the aims and desires of the world." More's friend, Erasmus, was of the opinion that it was the question of celibacy which turned More from the spiritual life. "When of a sentimental age, he was not a stranger to the emotions of love," he wrote, "but without loss of character, having no inclination to press his advantage, and being more attracted by a mutual liking than by any licentious object . . . he applied his whole mind to religion, having some thought of taking orders, for which he prepared himself by watchings and fastings and prayers and such like exercises; wherein he showed much more wisdom than the generality of people, who rashly engage in so arduous a profession without testing themselves beforehand. And indeed there was no obstacle to his adopting this kind of life, except the fact that he could not shake off his wish to marry. Accordingly he resolved to be a chaste husband rather than a licentious priest." [1]

In some support of Erasmus' statement that More "was not a stranger to the emotions of love" is a poem he wrote in later years, which was dedicated to an Elizabeth, whom apparently he knew when he was sixteen and she younger. In pretty verse he tells her that the years had passed since first they met but the memory of her remained with him.

Severed, our different fates we then pursued,
Till this late date my raptures has renewed.
Crimeless, my heart you stole in life's soft prime,
And still possess that heart without a crime.
Pure was the love which in my youth prevailed,
And age would keep it pure, if honour failed.
O may the gods, who, five long lustres passed,
Have brought us to each other well at last,
Grant, that when numbered five long lustres more,
Healthful, I still may hail thee healthful as before! [2]

"A chaste husband rather than a licentious priest." Once having decided to be a husband, More lost no time in finding a bride. A descendant of the union which he was soon to make, Cresacre More, declares that it was More's confessor who urged him to matrimony. He gives an account of a somewhat odd courtship: "Sir Thomas More having determined by the advice and direction of his ghostly father to be a married man, there was at that time a pleasant . . . gentleman of an ancient family in Essex, one Mr. John Colt . . . that invited him to his house, being much delighted in his company, and proffered unto him the choice of any of his daughters, who were young gentlewomen of very good carriage and complexions, and very religiously inclined, whose honest and sweet conversation, whose virtuous education enflamed Sir Thomas not a little; and although his affection most served him to the second, for that he thought her the fairest and best favoured; yet when he thought with himself, that this would be a grief and some blemish in the eldest to see her younger sister preferred before her, he, of a kind of compassion settled his fancy upon the eldest, and soon after married her, with all her friends good liking.[3]

The role of husband fitted Thomas More awkwardly at the beginning. Jane Colt was ten years his junior. The girl bride missed the companionship of her sisters and liked not at all the exchange of rustic peace for London tumult. The shy girl of seventeen must have had many a tremulous moment when asked to play hostess to such close friends of her husband's as the learned doctors, Grocyn and Linacre, and the Dutch scholar, Erasmus. Besides, More was fresh from the sombre company of the Carthusians. From childhood his companions had been elder and serious men. It is true there was that other and lighter side to his nature; he was the man of broad humour who later kept a clown in his house, and monkeys in his garden. But the many heavy excursions into philosophy and theology provided little charm for the new bride, and during the first days of their marriage she was bewildered and distressed.

Early during More's marriage Erasmus came from Rotterdam to visit the More household at Bucklersbury in London, and what he saw there provided him with the basis of a tale which he wrote years later. It was the story of a learned man who endeavoured to educate a young wife by "getting her to repeat the substance of the sermons she heard." Copious weepings and expressions of misery being the only result of such heavy instruction, the husband finally appealed to his father-in-law. "Use your rights," he was told, "and give her a good beating." When the husband refused to adopt such drastic measures, the father feigned such a rage and became so disagreeable that the frightened girl was glad to seek solace in the soothing arms of an understanding husband.

Whatever the reason, the adjustment to each other was quickly made, and with compatibility came an idyllic happiness. A child was expected and during the long wait the young wife cheerfully took lessons in music from her husband, and, with affectionate submission, made effort to share his learning and to absorb his teaching.

4

MORE'S fame as a scholar was steadily growing. He was a hospitable man, and there was a steady traffic of learned guests to awe young Mistress Jane.

"In London there are five or six men," wrote Desiderius Erasmus to Servatius on the occasion of his second visit to that city, "who are accurate scholars in both tongues, such as I think even Italy itself does not at present possess.[1]

The celebrated Hollander was about twelve years older than More, and a friendship spontaneously and quickly developed between them. This association was to prove immensely stimulating and valuable to two men who were able in many respects and with like interests, yet differed widely in character and conscience. They were peers in scholarship and wit, and, with More and Machiavelli,

Erasmus has been called a pioneer in political philosophy. Father Phillip Hughes agrees with Mesmard in declaring that as an influence in European life Erasmus won importance never achieved by any other writer, even Voltaire. Some writers have dubbed him "the Voltaire of the Renaissance," but in this they are mistaken, for Erasmus, while bitterly attacking a corrupt clergy was never, like the Frenchman, against the Church itself.

The circumstances which surrounded his birth and early life reflected his times and the need for that reform which employed the pen of both himself and More. He was the son of a priest, and while still a youth he had been thrust into a monastery without any true liking for the religious life. Monastic discipline proved terribly irksome, and the confining walls of a Priory of the Augustinian Canons were a harsh restraint to the vocationless lad who yearned to travel and to enjoy the delights of secular scholarship and classical research. A wise superior made it possible for him to leave the cloister and, as a Latin secretary, to secure employment in the household of the Bishop of Cambrai. His literary skill and productivity soon won him fame and the patronage and esteem of the great. Unlike most of his contemporaries, he was aware of the true significance of the printing press and the tremendous changes it was to bring. He became the most important leader of German Humanism, and because of his ceaseless and savage attacks on existing ecclesiastical conditions he has been charged with being the intellectual father of the Reformation. But unlike Luther, he never broke with Rome. He watched the revolt with interest, but he was appalled by the bigotry and ferocious intolerance of its leaders. He was a prodigy, but, alas, the possession of genius has never been a guaranty against the weaknesses of egotism and vanity. He was brilliant and discerning and utterly devoid of that strength of character which was so markedly the property of More.

Holbein shows him long-nosed and thin-lipped, cadaverous, and somewhat bland in expression, bent with the stoop of a scholar. He had pale blue eyes and, as Lindsay in his famed book on the Reformation remarks, "the dainty hands, and general primness of his appearance" suggested descent "from a long line of maiden aunts." Unhappy in his own ill-bestowed priesthood and ever cynical of the practice of formalized religion in others, he never, in his long friendship with More, found anything to criticize in the life and habits of one who rigidly adhered to the practices of his staunch faith.

More and Erasmus met, so legend has it, in the great hall where the Lord Mayor of London was accustomed to preside over a lavish banqueting table. The conversation and company fitted well the generous hospitality, and in the repartee that was exchanged the two scholars discovered the measure of each other. "You must be More or no one," cried the delighted Hollander. "You must be Erasmus or the Devil," was the reply from the Englishman.

Their intellectual prowess brought the two friends into exalted company, and from Erasmus we learn of a historic meeting with the future Henry VIII. More came to meet Erasmus, who was a guest in Lord Mountjoy's country house. They walked as far as the next village. ". . . there all the Royal children were being educated, Arthur alone excepted, the eldest son. When we came to the Hall, all the retinue was assembled; not only that of the palace, but Mountjoy's as well. In the midst stood Henry, aged nine, and having already something of royalty in his demeanour; in which there was a certain dignity combined with singular courtesy. On his right was Margaret, about eleven years old, who afterwards married James, King of Scots; and on his left played Mary, a child of four. Edmund was an infant in arms. More with his companion Arnold, after paying his respects to the boy Henry, the same that is now King of England, presented him with some writing."[2] The golden-haired boy looked at the two scholars with respect. Favoured by God in every way this most princely of princes was, in a very few years, to court the services of both. He, too, was to be dazzled by wide and splendid prospects of the New Learning, and it was their friend Linacre who was to teach him a workable knowledge of Latin within the brief span of six weeks.

Many years of friendship and even the crucible of literary collaboration did not lessen Erasmus' admiration for More. In a famous letter to Ulrich von Hutten the Hollander's talent and affection moulded a striking eulogy of his friend which invariably is, as it should be, quoted whenever a full-length portrait of More is sought: "Most illustrious Hutten—your love, I had almost said your passion for the genius of Thomas More, —kindled as it is by his writings, which, as you truly say, are as learned and witty as anything can possibly be, —is, I assure you, shared by many others; and moreover the feeling in this case is mutual; since More is so delighted with what you have written, that I am myself almost jealous of you. It is an example of what Plato says of that sweetest wisdom, which excites much more ardent love among men than the most admirable beauty of form. It is not discerned by the eye of sense, but the mind has eyes of its own, so that even here the Greek saying holds true, that out of Looking grows Liking; and so it comes to pass that people are sometimes united in the warmest affection, who have never seen or spoken to each other. And, as it is a common experience, that for some unexplained reason different people are attracted by different kinds of beauty, so between one mind and another, there seems to be a sort of latent kindred, which causes us to be specially delighted with some minds, and not with others.

"As to your asking me to paint you a full-length portrait of More, I only wish my power of satisfying your request were equal to your earnestness in pressing it. For me, too, it will be no unpleasant task to linger a while in the contemplation of a friend, who is the most delightful character in the world. But, in the first place, it is not given to every man to be aware of all More's accomplishments; and in the next place, I know not whether he will himself like to have his portrait painted by any artist that chooses to do so. For indeed I do not think it more easy to make a likeness of More than of Alexander the Great or of Achilles; neither were those heroes more worthy of immortality. The hand of an Apelles is required for such a subject, and I am afraid I am more like a Fulvius or a Rutuba than an Apelles. Nevertheless I will try to draw you a sketch, rather than a portrait of the entire man, so far as daily and domestic intercourse has enabled me to observe his likeness and retain it in my memory. But if some diplomatic employment should ever bring you together, you will find out, how poor an artist you have chosen for this commission; and I am afraid you will think me guilty of envy or of willful blindness in taking note of so few out of the many good points of his character.

"To begin with that part of him which is least known to you, —in shape and stature More is not a tall man, but not remarkably short, all his limbs being so symmetrical, that no deficiency is observed in this respect. His complexion is fair, being rather blonde than pale, but with no approach to redness, except a very delicate flush, which lights up the whole. His hair is auburn inclining to black, or if you like it better, black inclining to auburn; his beard thin, his eyes a bluish grey with some sort of tinting upon them. This kind of eye is thought to be a sign of the happiest character, and is regarded with favour in England, whereas with us black eyes are rather preferred. It is said, that no kind of eye is so free from defects of sight. His countenance answers to his character, having an expression of kind and friendly cheerfulness with a little air of raillery. To speak candidly, it is a face more expressive of pleasantry than of gravity or dignity, though very far removed from folly or buffoonery. His right shoulder seems a little higher than his left, especially when he is walking, a peculiarity that is not innate, but the result of habit, like many tricks of the kind. In the rest of his body there is nothing displeasing, only his hands are a little coarse, or appear so, as compared with the rest of his figure. He has always from his boyhood been very negligent of his toilet, so as not to give much attention even to the things which according to Ovid are all that men need care about. What a charm there was in his looks when young, may even now be inferred from what remains; although I knew him myself when he was not more than three-and-twenty years old; for he has not yet passed much beyond his fortieth year. His health is sound rather than robust, but sufficient for any labours suitable to an honourable citizen; and we may fairly hope that his life may be long, as he has a father living of a great age, but an age full of freshness and vigour.

"I have never seen any person less fastidious in his choice of food. As a young man, he was by preference a water-drinker, a practice he derived from his father. But, not to give annoyance to others, he used at table to conceal this habit from his guests by drinking, out of a pewter vessel, either small beer almost as weak as water, or plain water. As to wine, it being the custom, where he was, for the company to invite each other to drink in turn of the same cup, he used sometimes to sip a little of it, to avoid appearing to shrink from it altogether, and to habituate himself to the common practice. For his eating he has been accustomed to prefer beef and salt meats, and household bread thoroughly fermented to those articles of diet which are commonly regarded as delicacies. But he does not shrink from things that impart an innocent pleasure, even of a bodily kind, and has always a good appetite for milk puddings and for fruit, and eats a dish of eggs with the greatest relish.

"His voice is neither loud nor excessively low, but of a penetrating tone. It has nothing in it melodious or soft, but is simply suitable for speech, as he does not seem to have any natural talent for singing, though he takes pleasure in music of every kind. His articulation is wonderfully distinct, being equally free from hurry and from hesitation.

"He likes to be dressed simply, and does not wear silk,

or purple, or gold chains, except when it is not allowable
to dispense with them. He cares marvellously little for those
formalities which with ordinary people are the test of
politeness, and as he does not exact these ceremonies from
others, so he is not scrupulous in observing them himself,
either on occasions of meeting or at entertainments, though
he understands how to use them, if he thinks proper to do
so; but he holds it to be effeminate and unworthy of a man
to waste much of his time on such trifles. . .

"He seems to be born and made for friendship, of which
he is the sincerest and most persistent devotee. Neither is
he afraid of that multiplicity of friends, of which Hesiod
disapproves. Accessible to every tender of intimacy, he is
by no means fastidious in choosing his acquaintance, while
he is most accommodating in keeping it on foot, and constant in retaining it. If he has fallen in with anyone whose
faults he cannot cure, he finds some opportunity of parting
with him, untying the knot of intimacy without tearing it;
but when he has found any sincere friends, whose characters are suited to his own, he is so delighted with their
society and conversation, that he seems to find in these the
chief pleasure of life, having an absolute distaste for tennis
and dice and cards, and the other games with which the
mass of gentlemen beguile the tediousness of Time. It
should be added that, while he is somewhat neglectful of his
own interest, no one takes more pains in attending to the
concerns of his friends. What more need I say? If anyone
requires a perfect example of his true friendship, it is in
More that he will best find it.

"In company his extraordinary kindness and sweetness
of temper are such as to cheer the dullest spirit, and allevi-

ate the annoyance of the most trying circumstances. From boyhood he was always so pleased with a joke, that it might seem that jesting was the main object of his life; but with all that, he did not go so far as buffoonery, nor had ever any inclination to bitterness. When quite a youth, he wrote farces and acted them. If a thing was facetiously said, even though it was aimed at himself, he was charmed with it, so much did he enjoy any witticism that had a flavour of subtlety or genius. This led to his amusing himself as a young man with epigrams, and taking great delight in Lucian. Indeed, it was he that suggested my writing the *Moria,* or *Praise of Folly,* which was much the same thing as setting a camel to dance.

"There is nothing that occurs in human life, from which he does not seek to extract some pleasure, although the matter may be serious in itself. If he has to do with the learned and intelligent, he is delighted with their cleverness; if with unlearned or stupid people, he finds amusement in their folly. He is not offended even by professed clowns, as he adapts himself with marvellous dexterity to the tastes of all; while with ladies generally and even with his wife, his conversation is made up of humour and playfulness. You would say it was a second Democritus, or rather that Pythagorean philosopher, who strolls in leisurely mood through the marketplace, contemplating the turmoil of those who buy or sell. There is no one less guided by the opinion of the multitude, but on the other hand no one sticks more closely to common sense.

"One of his amusements is in observing the forms, characters and instincts of different animals. Accordingly, there is scarcely any kind of bird that he does not keep about his

residence, and the same of other animals not quite so common, as monkeys, foxes, ferrets, weasels, and the like.
Besides these, if he meets with any strange object, imported
from abroad or otherwise remarkable, he is most eager to
buy it, and has his house so well supplied with these
objects, that there is something in every room which catches
your eye, as you enter it; and his own pleasure is renewed
every time that he sees others interested. . .

"His house seems to have a sort of fatal felicity, no one
having lived in it without being advanced to higher fortune,
no inmate having ever had a stain upon his character.

"It would be difficult to find anyone living on such terms
with a mother as he does with his stepmother. For his father
had brought in one stepmother after another; and he has
been as affectionate with each of them as with a mother.
He has lately introduced a third, and More swears that he
never saw anything better. His affection for his parents,
children and sisters is such, that he neither wearies them
with his love, nor ever fails in any kind attention.

"His character is entirely free from any touch of avarice.
He has set aside out of his property what he thinks sufficient for his children, and spends the rest in a liberal
fashion. When he was still dependent on his profession, he
gave every client true and friendly counsel, with an eye to
their advantage rather than his own, generally advising
them, that the cheapest thing they could do was to come
to terms with their opponents. If he could not persuade
them to do this, he pointed out how they might go to law
at least expense; for there are some people whose character
leads them to delight in litigation. . . .

"It has always been part of his character to be most

obliging to everybody, and marvellously ready with his sympathy; and this disposition is more conspicuous than ever, now that his power of doing good is greater. Some he relieves with money, some he protects by his authority, some he promotes by his recommendation, while those whom he cannot otherwise assist are benefited by his advice. No one is sent away in distress, and you might call him the general patron of all poor people. He counts it a great gain to himself, if he has relieved some oppressed person, made the path clear for one that was in difficulties, or brought back into favour one that was in disgrace. No man more readily confers a benefit, no man expects less in return. And successful as he is in so many ways—while success is generally accompanied by self-conceit, I have never seen any mortal being more free from this failing.

"I now propose to turn to the subject of those studies which have been the chief means of bringing More and me together. In his first youth his principal literary exercises were in verse. He afterwards wrestled for a long time to make his prose more smooth; practising his pen in every kind of writing in order to form that style, the character of which there is no occasion for me to recall, especially to you, who have his books always in your hands. He took the greatest pleasure in declamations, choosing some disputable subject, as involving a keener exercise of mind. Hence, while still a youth, he attempted a dialogue, in which he carried the defence of Plato's community even to the matter of wives! He wrote in answer to Lucian's *Tyrannicide,* in which argument it was his wish to have me for a rival, in order to test his own proficiency in this kind of writing.

"He published his *Utopia* for the purpose of showing what are the things that occasion mischief in commonwealths; having the English constitution especially in view, which he so thoroughly knows and understands. He had written the second book at his leisure, and afterwards, when he found it was required, added the first off-hand. Hence there is some inequality in the style.

"It would be difficult to find anyone more successful in speaking *ex tempore,* the happiest thoughts being attended by the happiest language; while a mind that catches and anticipates all that passes, and a ready memory, having everything as it were in stock, promptly supply whatever the time, or the occasion, demands. In disputations nothing can be imagined more acute, so that the most eminent theologians often find their match, when he meets them on their own ground. Hence John Colet, a man of keen and exact judgment, is wont to say in familiar conversation, that England has only one genius, whereas that island abounds in distinguished intellects.

"However averse he may be from all superstition, he is a steady adherent of true piety; having regular hours for his prayers, which are not uttered by rote, but from the heart. He talks with his friends about a future life in such a way as to make you feel that he believes what he says, and does not speak without the best hope. Such is More, even at Court; and there are still people who think that Christians are only to be found in monasteries!"[3]

5

ONCE Thomas More was certain that the way of the Carthusians was not for him, he not only applied himself to his profession but also turned his attention to public affairs. In the beginning of the year 1504 he was elected to the House of Commons "for many had now taken notice of his sufficiency." He was only twenty-four, but immediately he won celebrity by raising an eloquent voice against the wishes of the King. It was risky business, this opposition to a cunning ruler whose avarice and greed matched his dynastic ambitions.

Henry VII had convened this parliament to extort money in the form of "reasonable aids, on the occasion of the marriage of his daughter and the knighting of his son." The royal request was in accord with feudal practice, but the subsidy demanded was preposterously high, one hundred and thirteen thousand pounds. This at a time when: "a fat ox sold for twenty-six shillings, and a chicken bought for a penny." The son, Prince Arthur, was already dead, and it was certain that even if Parliament did accede to Henry's wishes, his daughter would not carry a too extravagant dowry to her Scottish spouse. Nevertheless, a docile Commons probably would have submitted if young Thomas More had not rallied and strengthened the opposition. He spoke with the audacity of youth, the brilliance of a natural orator, and the logic of an adept practitioner of the law.

His words stirred the hearts of his older colleagues. Their courage mounted. They rejected the King's exorbitant demands, and though a grant was finally voted, it was less than one third of the original request. A Mr. Tyler, one of the King's Privy Chamber, did what was expected of him and rushed to Henry with the information that "a beardless boy had disappointed all his purpose. Whereupon the King, conceiving great indignation towards him, could not be satisfied until he had some way revenged it."[1]

Tudor revenge was notoriously prompt and fierce, but on this occasion, for some reason, the irascible monarch bided his time. Perhaps the knowledge of law that his young antagonist had displayed before Parliament made the wily prince seek some form of legality. He gave a long and thorough look at the Mores, father and son, and on a trumped-up charge had the father arrested and imprisoned in the Tower until a fine of a hundred pounds was levied and paid.

More and his friends were alarmed. He thought of fleeing the country, and with exile in mind, he began to study

French and to withdraw from his practice at the bar. That he had good cause for fear is shown in his son-in-law's account of the following incident. According to Roper, More brought a suit to Dr. Fox, Bishop of Winchester, a member of the King's Privy Counsel. The Bishop called him aside, "and pretending great favour towards him, promised him that, if he would be ruled by him he would not fail into the King's favour again to restore him, —meaning (as it was after conjectured), to cause him thereby to confess his offenses against the King, whereby His Highness might with the better colour have occasion to revenge his displeasure against him. But when he came from the Bishop, he fell into communication with one Master Whitford, his familiar friend, then chaplain to that Bishop . . . and showed him what the Bishop had said unto him, desiring to have his advice, therein; who for the passion of God, prayed him in no wise to follow his counsel: 'For my Lord, my master,' quoth he, 'to serve the King's turn, will not stick to agree to his own father's death.' "[2]

More did not return to the Bishop again, nor did he make any confessions to the King. How wise was this friendly counsel may be deduced from the legendary account of the two notorious unfortunates, Dudley and Empson. Upon being led to their execution, Dudley spied More and cried: "Oh, More, More! God was your good friend that you did not ask the King forgiveness, as many would have had you do, for if you had done so, perhaps you should have been in the like case with us now."[3]

During the year that preceded the death of Henry VII, More crossed the Channel, ostensibly to transact legal affairs on behalf of a group of merchants, but, in the interests of prudence, he probably was also seeking a suitable refuge in case he had to flee. While on the Continent he visited the universities of Louvain and Paris. Seven years later he described that visit in a letter to Martin Dorp: "I was in both those universities and though not for a very long time, yet I took pains to ascertain what was taught there and what methods were followed. Though I respect both of them, yet neither from what I saw then, nor from what I have since heard, have I found any reason why, even in dialectics, I should wish any sons of mine (for whom I desire the very best education) to be taught there rather than at Oxford or Cambridge."[4]

The projected exile did not materialize, for the King died and the hostilities of his reign were pushed to the past even while the candles of his requiem still burned. His son took the throne. "Vive le Roy!" cried the chief herald, and all England, released from the strain of the old King, joyfully acclaimed the name of Henry the Eighth.

A new era was promised in the splendid person of this magnificent boy. Tall and handsome, rich in intellect, rich in power, rich in purse, eager for learning, eager for justice, the eighteen-year-old prince embodied the hopes of an entire nation. The most discerning eye could yet not detect in the broad-shouldered, spectacularly beautiful youth any trace of the besotted tyrant, the cruel butcher, the lustful libertine.

At his side was Wolsey, already splendid, already rich, already chaplain to the young monarch, soon to be Almoner, planning the first of his great mansions, lifting his eyes to the scarlet, happy in his dreams of power.

Happy too was sombre-eyed little Catherine of Aragon.

It was nearly seven long years since the Spanish Princess had landed at Plymouth amidst the gaudy flutter of Spanish standards and the welcome of English bells. It had not been easy for her in this strange land. Her Spanish ways and her Spanish retinue were often regarded with suspicion. Even More wrote of her court: "You would have burst with laughing if you had seen them. They looked like devils out of Hell." But in the same letter he gave voice to a loyalty to Catherine which was never to wane. "There is nothing wanting in her, that the most beautiful girl should have . . . May this famous marriage be fortunate and of good omen to England."[5]

The young Princess, puppet of dynasts and courts, had obediently accepted her betrothed, Arthur, the King's first son. He was younger than she, and a sickly creature. Upon her marriage to the frail boy her escort to the altar had been his younger brother Henry, then a sturdy ten-year-old youngster, intended by his penurious father for the Church and the revenues of Canterbury. But the royal union had never been consummated. Within a few months Arthur was dead, and again the fate of the Princess became the shuttle-cock of dynasts. One hundred thousand crowns, half of her dowry, had been paid into the coffers of Henry VII, and he had no intention of returning it. Many decisions, not helped by the slow communication with the Spanish court, had to be made. The tacticians maneuvered with exasperating procrastination, and the young girl, tremulous with the aches of homesickness and uncertainty, bowed to their discipline. At length a dispensation had been procured from Pope Julius II to allow her to marry her husband's brother. The betrothal was solemnly made official, but the English King had demurred and postponed the wedding, intently scanning the shifting and complicated course of the Toledo court, carefully weighing the advantages against the disadvantages of a Spanish alliance.

The negotiation with Rome had also been slow. The watchful ladies of Catherine's little court, so close to her in person and thoughts, were fiercely willing to swear that the marriage had never been consummated; that the nuptial bed of the sick boy and innocent girl had meant nothing. Nevertheless, the proceedings, delayed by the deaths of two Popes, had dragged on until the urgent appeals of Queen Isabella resulted in a Brief which was privately dispatched to Spain. Later a Bull of a more public character was promulgated. During these happenings, so important to her destiny, her father-in-law kept Catherine and her retinue in a seclusion marked by parsimonious restrictions and in an atmosphere of uncertainty and rumour. He also kept a firm grip on that portion of her dowry which had already been paid. The death of his wife, Elizabeth of York, following the delivery of their eighth child, created a new situation. Five of the children were already dead. There remained two daughters and but one son. The entire fortunes of the Tudor dynasty depended upon the life of this boy prince. Henry was forty-six, and not unreasonably he thought of another marriage and more sons to ensure the succession. His eyes for a short time turned upon Catherine, but from Spain came indignant objections and a suggestion instead that he choose a more fitting spouse in the person of the widowed Queen of Naples. With fairly good grace he then abandoned the somewhat unsavory plan of uniting himself with Catherine and agreed she should marry his remaining son.

Henry VII died on April 21, 1509, and in the clement days of May was lowered to his grave in kingly splendour. Not so regal was the wedding which followed nine weeks later, for, while Catherine worried and waited, a council had deliberated on her worth in the game of politics. There were those who favoured alliance with Spain and there were those who would rather seek friendship with France. One of the latter was the Archbishop of Canterbury, and he was willing to protest the papal dispensation and thus invoke the Levitical law. During the preceding intrigue the young Henry had secretly been taken before a bishop and instructed to protest his betrothal. But in the shadows of his father's deathbed, he had also solemnly vowed to follow the parental wish. He kept that promise, and soon, at the oratory of the Franciscan Observants in Greenwich, Catherine finally became England's Queen, joined to Henry by the very prelate who had wished to question the validity of the dispensation.

All England extravagantly welcomed the new King. All men lived in a joyful anticipation of a happy and enlightened reign. But no men were more happy than the scholars who comprised the advocates of the New Learning. They knew of the new sovereign's enlightened views and his sympathy for their speculations. It was certain that in his person they now had an ardent and enthusiastic patron. The thrill of the chase, the excitement of the jousting ground and gaming tables, the gossip of the court were not sufficient for the monarch. Mountjoy joyously reported to Erasmus that the young king had expressed his wish that he was more learned.

"That is not what we expect of your grace," answered Mountjoy, "but that you will foster and encourage learned men."

"Yea surely," came the humble reply, "for indeed without them we should scarcely exist at all."[6]

Henry's scholarship and his desire for even more knowledge was surprising. He had a working knowledge of Latin. His theology was better than that of many in orders. Astronomy fascinated him and the science of geometry did not repel him. He could discuss Aquinas with the same ease that he could compose a tune or fashion a couplet. The golden-haired youth was also a poet. In these early days of his reign (when Anne Boleyn was still in her cradle) he wrote of constancy:

> Green groweth the holly, so doth the ivy
> Though winter blasts blow never so high,
> Green groweth the holly.
>
> As the holly groweth green
>   And never changeth hue,
> So I am, ever have been,
>   Unto my lady true.[7]

The advent of the new regime lifted the heavy weight that had oppressed Thomas More during the latter years of the reign of Henry VII. Because of his bold action in Parliament, the hardships and uncertainty of exile had been a very active threat while the old king had lived. A new life in a new country might not have been too irksome for a bachelor, but in 1509 More was not only a husband but a father. Since his marriage to Jane Colt in 1505, four children had arrived, three girls and one son. Margaret was the eldest, then came Elizabeth and Cecilia and finally his only son, John. Inevitably parenthood widened the scope of his affections, but the broad vista of family love was clouded by responsibility. The enthronement of the enlightened young King dissipated the dismal likelihood of flight abroad. Thomas More was now able to speak his mind and practice his profession. The joy in his heart inspired him to hail the youthful sovereign in the lyrical lines of a Latin poem, in which he enumerated the virtues of Henry and his ancestors; the noble heart of his grandfather, Edward IV; the piety of his grandmother, the Lady Margaret; the kindliness of his mother, Elizabeth of York; the prudence of his father, Henry VII; nor did he omit Queen Catherine, whom he compared to the faithful Greek wives, Alcestis and Penelope. In concluding his verses, More dwelt on the son whom Catherine was to bear Henry to perpetuate his dynasty, and in so doing the poet proved a poor prophet, as he himself must have ruefully confessed to himself in the sad years that terminated the royal marriage.

But in 1509 Henry's subjects rejoiced in the death of tyranny and the rebirth of liberty. Mountjoy dispatched a letter to his old teacher, Erasmus, who was then in Italy, inviting him to return to England:

"Oh, my Erasmus," he wrote, "if you could see how all the world here is rejoicing in the possession of so great a prince, how his life is all their desire, you could not contain your tears for joy. . . Avarice is expelled the country. Liberality scatters wealth with bounteous hand. Our King does not desire gold or gems or precious metals, but virtue, glory, immortality . . . Make up your mind that the last day of your wretchedness has dawned. . . You will come to a Prince who will say, 'Accept our wealth and be our greatest sage.' "8

Erasmus had mounted far on the ladder of success since his first meeting with More. His name was held in high esteem throughout Europe and he was regarded as the foremost oracle of his time. He was welcome at the tables of rulers and high prelates, but because of the promise inherent in the reign of the young English monarch, he joyfully accepted Mountjoy's invitation to return to England and share in the blessings of the new reign.

To while away the tedium of the long journey from Italy to England, most of which was made on horseback, Erasmus composed his famous panegyric, *Moriae Encomium,* or *The Praise of Folly.* In the epistle to More which served as the dedication to the work, Erasmus confessed that he was prompted to write the *Moriae* by the resemblance between More's family name and the Greek word for "fool." "In the next place I surmised, that this playful production of our genius would find special favour with you, disposed as you are to take pleasure in jests of this kind, —jests, which, I trust, are neither ignorant nor quite insipid, —and generally in society, to play a sort of Democritus. . . You will therefore not only willingly receive this little declamation, as a memento of your comrade, but will adopt and protect it, as dedicated to you, and become not mine, but yours."9

The actual writing of the book was done in More's house. On his arrival, Erasmus suffered an acute attack of lumbago. Having none of his own books at hand, he occupied himself in setting his *Moriae* on paper.

In April, 1511, Erasmus, tired of waiting for favours that never came, left England for Paris, where was published his *Moriae Encomium*. It promptly went into seven editions. But Erasmus, like More in his panegyric to the young King, had overshot his mark. *The Praise of Folly* was a denunciation on the part of the Humanists of the evils of their time. It decried the dishonesty and irreverence among clericals, the methods of Biblical interpretation used by scholars, the irresponsibilities and vaingloriousness of rulers, and other blatant social evils. The object was reform, but the tone was light, and *Moriae* furnished heavy ammunition for those who questioned authority, and particularly the authority of Rome. Thomas More was too closely identified with the *Moriae* to escape criticism. On being charged with aiding irreverence, he refuted the charge and defended Erasmus, at one and the same time.

"Nor if there were any such thing in *Moriae,* that thing could not yet make any man see that I were myself of that mind, the book being made by another man, though he were my darling never so dear. Howbeit, that book of *Moriae* doth indeed but jest upon the abuses of such things, after the manner of the jester's part in a play."[10]

For more than two years Erasmus waited hopefully for a summons from Henry VIII to return to England. Finally, John Fisher, Chancellor of Cambridge University, persuaded him to come to the University to lecture in Greek. In September, 1513, Erasmus took refuge from the plague

with his friends the Gunnells at Landbeach. In the beginning of January, 1514, he determined to leave England. He
returned to the continent and settled at Basle.

More had assiduously applied himself to the business of
law. Success came with remarkable quickness, and soon he
was the recipient of an annual income, according to Roper,
that exceeded four hundred pounds. It is difficult to judge
the worth of money from one age to the next, but one may
hazard the estimate that More's income, compared with
modern standards, approximated one hundred thousand
dollars per year. So great were the demands made upon
him. ". . . there was at that time in none of the Princes'
Courts of the laws of this realm," recorded his son-in-law,
"any matter of importance in controversy wherein he was
not with the one part of counsel."[11]

His hours were crowded, yet he found time to accept an
appointment as Under-Sheriff of London, a judicial office
of no small importance. More performed the duties of his
office every Thursday morning and held it to be a high
honour. He was careful but quick in his decisions, and there
was a great traffic in his court. He was just, he had wide
knowledge of the law, and often when the litigants were
poor he remitted the fees due him. The care and skill and
wisdom which More displayed as a judge did much to win
him the esteem and popularity of his fellow citizens, and
it also gave him a valuable and profound schooling in human nature.

Success at the bar was matched by domestic tranquillity.
The little misunderstandings between the bride and groom,
the scholar and the country miss, had vanished after six

years of marriage. Jane had now some understanding of
her husband's bent and was not afraid of his distinguished
friends. She had learned to perform on the viol and she
could sing prettily. Like most young parents she and her
husband dreamed of, and made plans for, a larger residence.

Her husband had definite and elaborate ideas for the
education of his children. They were all to be scholars.
The girls were not to be exempted because of their sex
for, unlike most of his contemporaries, he held enlightened
views on the position and education of women.

"Nor do I think that the harvest will be much affected
whether it is a man or a woman who sows the field. They
both have the same human nature, which reason differen-
tiates from that of beasts; both therefore are equally suited
for those studies by which reason is perfectioned, and be-
comes fruitful like a ploughed land on which the seed of
good lessons has been sown. If it be true that the soil of
woman's brain be bad, and apter to bear bracken than corn,
by which saying many keep women from study, I think,
on the contrary, that a woman's wit is on that account all
the more diligently to be cultivated, that nature's defect
may be redressed by industry."[12]

With tender care his theory had been given practice with
his wife. Throughout the long months of one pregnancy
after another, he had moulded her young mind to an appreciation of the delights of the intellect. But it was not all
sombre study. There was singing and there were games
and there was much romping with the children. There was
great joy in the More household, and oftentimes he was

disturbed because of the long hours which his profession forced him to spend away from his hearth.

He held a particular devotion to his firstborn, Margaret, which was never to waver and which always was to be reciprocated. "Meg" was his pet name for her, and as the eldest child she was the first to undergo his carefully prepared training. She was taught Latin, Greek, Logic, Philosophy, Theology, Mathematics, and Astronomy. It was a formidable course upon which to embark a young girl, but its terrors were lightened by the charm and humour and genius of More's personal direction and understanding.

Margaret was only five years old and her young brother not yet a year when their mother, the sweet-natured Jane, suddenly died.

Before a month passed More married again. It was a deliberate action. He had four young children, three of whom were girls, in his house. Professional tasks and civic duties occupied most of his hours. No matter how scrupulously and carefully he acted the father, there still remained the necessity of a mother's care. With this thought in mind he chose a widow, seven years older than himself, Mistress Alice Middleton. Of her children by her first husband, one, Alice, was young enough to be brought up with More's children. It was a practical arrangement, this union. His second wife was a good woman and an efficient housekeeper, although she was never able to attain a full understanding of the many sides of her husband's character. Years later Father Bouge, More's parish priest, wrote of the suddenness of the second marriage: "I buried his first wife. And within a month after, he came to me on a Sunday, at night, late, and there he brought me a dispensation to be married the next Monday, without any banns asking . . . This Mr. More was my ghostly child: in his confession to be so pure, so clean, with great study, deliberation, and devotion, I never heard many such. . ."[13]

Jane, the mother of his children, was never forgotten by More. Nearly twenty years later, when he made ready for his own burial, he had her coffin transferred to the grave he thought he would occupy. He wrote his epitaph and in his graceful Latin she took her place as "dear Jane, Thomas More's little wife."

By the time he had reached his thirty-fifth birthday, Thomas More had achieved a state of living that would have satisfied the aims of most men. He was a lawyer with a wide and lucrative practice. As Under-Sheriff he had gained an envied position in the City of London. He was a popular Bencher amongst his colleagues at Lincoln's Inn. He was an acknowledged scholar with a large circle of distinguished friends. He was a fond parent and a considerate husband.

His every hour was apportioned to a duty or a task, and he was jealous of inconsequentialities that diverted or stole his time. He thought he was neglecting his literary work. In a letter to his friend Peter Giles he complained: "For while in pleading, in hearing, in deciding causes, or composing disputes as an arbitrator, in waiting on some men about business, and on others out of respect, the greatest part of the day is spent on other men's affairs, the remainder of it must be given to my family at home; so that I can reserve no part to myself, that is, to study. I must gossip with my wife and chat with my children, and find something to say to

CATHERINE OF ARAGON

my servants; for all these things I reckon a part of my business, unless I were to become a stranger in my house; for with whomsoever either nature or choice or chance has engaged a man in any relation of life, he must endeavour to make himself as acceptable to them as he possibly can. In such occupations as these, days, months, and years slip away. Indeed all the time which I can gain to myself is that which I steal from my sleep and my meals, and because that is not much I have made but a slow progress."[14]

He made no mention of the long hours he gave to religious exercises. Every morning saw him at Mass. Every day this busy lawyer recited prayers and read the Psalms with his household. He made numerous pilgrimages, and in the interest of self-discipline he underwent austerities that were worthy of the monastery. He was always reticent about this phase of his life, this taming of the flesh. Even when he became Lord Chancellor of the realm he wore beneath the splendid robe of office a hair shirt that chafed and bloodied his body.

The act of penance was confided to his beloved elder daughter Margaret, and it was she who washed the penitential garment. She was capable of understanding such asceticism, unlike his wife, who strongly disapproved.

Dame Alice could not comprehend the mortification that induced More to wear the hair shirt as antidote to his material success and outward comfort. She went to his confessor and voiced her alarm. "His wife," wrote the priest, "desired me to counsel him to put off that hard and rough shirt of hair: and yet it is very long, almost a twelve-month, ere she knew of this habergeon of hair; it tamed his flesh till the blood was seen in his clothes."[15]

More first wore the hair shirt when he was at Oxford, and it was a penance never abandoned. Years after Dame Alice's complaint there is another incident. The heat of a summer day caused More to wear a plain shirt without ruff or collar. A hint of the hair shirt caught the alert eyes of his young daughter-in-law, Anne Cresacre. The girl was amused, but the ever attentive Margaret, according to her husband, "perceiving the same, privily told him of it; and he, being sorry that she saw it, presently amended it." More did not cease the penance until his execution was certain. Then from his cell in the Tower, the hair shirt was sent to Margaret with his last letter.

6

DESPITE More's lamentations that he had scant opportunity for literary activity, his pen was constantly engaged. In his thirty-fifth year we have seen that he was a busy man at law, yet this is the year he produced *The History of King Richard III*, the last of the House of York, and like everything of his invention it was composed with care. He wrote both in Latin and English, yet curiously enough *The History* was never finished. It could scarcely have been because he thought it was without merit. It was too good for that. The spirit which drives an author and buoys his dream could not have deserted him with such abruptness. Either he lacked the leisure to complete this excellent work, or, perhaps, he felt the need of caution in dealing with matters that might offend his young sovereign.

More's style in the Latin version has been likened to that of Tacitus, and it is generally acknowledged that in the vernacular it was the first and best history of its kind for many generations. He planned that it should be a history of his age. It was both a criticism of the structure of government and attack against the evils of tyrants. The eloquent prose was to give Shakespeare inspiration and material for his *Richard III,* and the mood of its theme was to provide its own author with the spirit that was responsible for *Utopia.*

The pitiable state of the common man, and the dire need for a new system of society, had long been the subject uppermost in the thoughts of More and his Humanist friends. The promise and person of the young Henry provided a bright hope, but in the fifth year of his reign there were already signs of the dark and brutal route that lay ahead.

This year of 1513 was the year of Flodden and of the invasion of France. Aided, and indeed prompted, by Wolsey, the young king was giving way to his martial dreams and grandiose schemes. The genius of Wolsey had brought forth the organization of a great army, the formation of a new fleet. The delights that Henry had found in philosophy and religion receded before the more active thrills of drum and cannon. The tramp of his soldiery, the booming salutes of his ships, intoxicated the young prince. Wearing his scarlet and gold, he paraded his warriors and lived in gleeful anticipation of conquest and victory. While the little group of Humanists frowned and worried, Henry played with his fleet as a child with his toys. He had his portrait painted on the deck of a ship of war. He delighted in his title of Supreme Head of the King's Navy Royal, and, as such, trumpeted on a large gold whistle. His ships answered in reverberating salute. He gave these gaily painted, well-bannered craft pretty and brave names. There were the *Dragon*, the *Lion*, the *Mary Rose*, the *Mary George*, the *Mary John*, the *George of Falmouth*, the *Anne of Greenwich*, the *Peter Pomegranate*. With a side glance at the scholars, one little vessel was named *Erasmus*.

The pretext for war was accompanied with an easy conscience that was soon to become familiar to England's King. Henry named some of his cannon after the Apostles, for this quarrel with France was, according to him, a Holy War. In crossing the Channel he actually was defending the Church and freeing it, so he proclaimed, "from the savage King of the French, who is the common enemy of all Christian princes."

The war with the Scots was also, according to his thinking, "a just, holy and somewhat necessary war," for the Scottish king in addition to his friendship with the French, had spoken against "the sovereign pontif, the head of our religion."

Giving support to these pious exclamations, always giving encouragement to the King's every whim, bowing, twisting, manipulating, entrenching himself in favour and power, wearing the cloth but prompting the sword, was the priest Wolsey, already rich in benefices and hungry for more, the patient and able architect of the new reign. His dreams now had dazzling scope. With this impetuous prince as instrument, England could become master of Europe, and on that grand scale England's destiny seemed to be his own fate. In his thoughts the cardinalitial splendour was a certainty, the tiara even not improbable.

More's good friend, Dean Colet, did not hesitate to voice open disapproval of the martial policies when he preached before Henry on Good Friday of 1513. His sermon was a bold attack on the evils of war and the wickedness of those who waged war. The King sent for him that very afternoon, and with some trepidation the Dean answered the summons. But the young monarch was all humility. He professed great piety and said he was in accord with Colet's sermon. Most wars were born of man's hatred and ambition, he agreed, but surely on occasion there was need for good men to defend that which was right. The Dean could not gainsay this logic, and then Henry in the same pious and humble vein, and with all his charm, explained that the French were definitely schismatics and enemies of the Church. This war was in truth a just war, and surely the good Dean would so mention in his next sermon. Colet murmured his surrender and received a royal embrace. The King called for wine and proposed Colet's health, "Let every one have his own doctor," he said, "and let every one favour his own; this man is the doctor for me."[1]

Back on the Continent, the disillusioned Erasmus voiced his disgust. "I often wonder," he wrote, "what thing it is that drives, I will not say Christians, but men, to such a degree of madness as to rush with so much pains, so much cost, so much risk, to the destruction of one another! . . . For us, who glory in the name of Christ . . . can anything in the world be of so great concern as to provoke us to war, a thing so calamitous and so hateful, that even when it is most righteous, no truly good man can approve it."[2]

While More was sharing with Colet and Erasmus this deep hatred of war and passion for peace, his fine legal training and his personal charm were attracting the attention of Wolsey, whose great schemes needed able men. More's talents were too pronounced to escape the attention of so alert a prelate. There were difficulties between the merchants of London and those of Flanders, and More was appointed to an embassy which was to represent the English interest. In the early summer of 1515 the envoys made their departure from England, and it was with heavy heart that the home-loving More said farewell to his family. Accompanying him as a fellow envoy was his friend, Cuthbert Tunstall, later to be Bishop of London. In addition to their royal credentials they carried a letter of introduction from Erasmus addressed to Peter Giles, the Town Clerk of Antwerp. He described More and Tunstall as being "the two most learned men of all England . . . both great friends of mine. If you should have an opportunity of offering them any civility, your services will be well bestowed."[3]

Another to travel with them was Richard Sampson, who represented Wolsey. Henry's armies had taken the town of Tournay from the French, and promptly Wolsey had acquired the bishopric of that region. Sampson was appointed his Vicar General, despite the resentment and objections of both Flemings and French, and he was instructed to impose his claims with vigorous authority, while at the same time wearing the cloak of diplomatic immunity. "Handle the matter boldly," he was ordered by his acquisitive master, "and fulminate the censures, not fearing for any excommunication of any man."

In More's mind the ambassadorial honour was poor compensation for leaving his family. There was also the question of expense. His lucrative legal practice naturally suffered during his absence, and he had no other revenues. "When I am away, I have two households to maintain, one in England and another abroad. I received a liberal allowance from the King for the persons I took with me, but no account is taken of those whom I leave at home." More's typical humour shows in this same letter. "Although you know what a kind husband, what an indulgent father, what a considerate master I am, yet I have never been able to induce my family to go without food during my absence. . ."[4]

He expected his stay abroad would not be more than sixty days, but because of the Tournay troubles the negotiations dragged, and he was gone for six months. His own finances reached a critical state. Tunstall reported to Wolsey: "Master More at this time, as being at a low ebb, desires by Your Grace to be set on float again."[5] Most of his time abroad was spent in the cities of Bruges, Brussels, and Antwerp, and it was during this period that the imaginary island of *Utopia* was given design.

The seed that Erasmus had planted with his letter of introduction to Peter Giles flowered into a companionship which was rich in intellectual productivity. The Englishman and his new friend utilized the long waits necessary to official duties by constantly discussing and analyzing the problems that agitated them. These talks and an appreciation of the wide attention given Erasmus' *The Praise of Folly* certainly did much to provide More with the inspiration to employ his pen in tracing his own conception of the reforms and philosophy necessary to an ideal commonwealth.

Utopia is divided into two books. The first book, which was written last and in more haste, was completed in 1516, the year of publication. It consists of a thinly disguised account of the wrongs that existed in the England of More's day. The second book, completed a year before, is a brilliant *jeu d'esprit*. For the amusement of his friends More took an idea—the idea of a society ruled by reason without Revelation—and followed where the idea led him. The Utopians are without Revelation, and for More, Revelation is essential to the conduct of life. With only reason to guide them—and not Reason in the abstract but their own fallible reason—they can but do their best: let us see what their best is, says More. He keeps a straight face, but amusement is the point. Every so often seriousness breaks in, mainly where indignation at contemporary contrasts is too strong for him. The moment over, he resumes the straight face and the brilliant fantasy. One imagines how the humourless learned have misread the book ever since. No one can be certain where this powerful, humorous mind is merely enjoying itself, where it is wholly serious. The natural tendency is to assume that More meant it, whenever he describes the Utopians doing something the reader agrees with. It is a highly unsafe rule, and has led to results as funny as anything in *Utopia*.

More began *Utopia* in an apparently realistic vein. He describes how his official duties took him to Antwerp, where he met Peter Giles, "a man of . . . honest reputation . . . Upon a certain day when I had heard the divine service in our Ladies Church I chanced to espy this . . . Peter talking with a certain stranger, a man well stricken in age, with a black sunburned face, a long beard, and a cloak cast homely about his shoulders, whom, by his favour and apparel forthwith I judged to be a mariner."[6] But More meets the stranger and finds him to be no mariner but a Portuguese philosopher with a liking for travel. He is Raphael Hythlodaye, the admiring observer of *Utopia*. The traveller tells his attentive listeners that he had accompanied the famous Amerigo Vespucci on his last three voyages. He had not returned with the explorer on the final voyage but had elected to stay with some companions on the coast of Brazil, and from that distant region he had slowly journeyed to Ceylon and Calicut and from thence home. He had seen many strange things and odd people. More invites him to a garden seat and the fabulous account begins.

There was ample reason to connect the story with the voyages of Amerigo Vespucci. Europe was then excited with the inviting horizons of the New World. Before More had attained his majority John Cabot had anchored off the American mainland. Before Henry VIII had ascended the throne, the chant of Sebastian Cabot's leadsmen, proclaiming their fathoms, had echoed over the cold waters of what we now call Hudson Bay. Returning navigators had strange stories to relate, and not the least of these tales was the legend of a civilized and prosperous people who held property in common and who, unlike Europeans, did not struggle for gold or gems. Even while *Utopia* was being written, More's brother-in-law, John Rastell, with the help of the More family, was organizing a colonization venture. Eventually his ship, the *Barbara*, left Greenwich, but the voyage failed because of a mutiny. The ambition remained in the family, and at a later date his son, John, crossed the ocean and landed in Labrador.

More's main interest, however, centered nearer home. His opinion of the King's service is clearly expressed early in the first book. Hythlodaye's listeners are impressed by his knowledge and wisdom, and Peter Giles puts him the question: "Surely Master Raphael . . . I wonder greatly, why you get you not into some king's court. For I am sure, there is no prince living that would not be very glad of you, as a man not only able highly to delight him with your profound learning and this your knowledge of countries and peoples, but also meet to instruct him with examples, and help him with counsel."[7] Hythlodaye replies that he has no wish to give himself in "bondage to Kings," and when further pressed says: "For, first of all, the most part of all princes have more delight in warlike matters and feats of chivalry (the knowledge whereof I neither have nor desire) than in the good feats of peace, and employ much more study how by right or wrong to enlarge their dominions, than how well and peaceably to rule and govern that they have already . . ."[8] Later he remarks bitterly that philosophy has "no place amongst Kings."

The dialogue continues. Existing conditions and injustices are discussed. Hythlodaye relates of the Utopians: "Among whom with very few laws, all things be so well and wealthily ordered, that virtue is had in price and estimation, and yet, all things being there common, every man hath abundance of everything." He agrees with Plato: "and do nothing marvel that he would make no laws for them, that refused those laws, whereby all men should have and enjoy equal portions of wealth and commodities. For the wise man did easily foresee this to be the one and only way to the wealth of a commonalty, if equality of all things should be brought in and established. Which I think is not possible to be observed, where every man's goods be proper and peculiar to himself . . . Thus I do fully persuade myself, that no equal and just distribution of things can be made . . . unless this property be exiled and banished . . ."

More disagrees: "Methinketh that men shall never there live wealthily, where all things be common. For how can there be abundance of goods, or of anything, where every man withdraweth his hand from labour? Whom the regard of his own gains driveth not to work, but the hope that he hath in other men's travail maketh him slothful . . ." [9]

Hythlodaye assures him that such a system works well in Utopia, whereupon More beseeches him to "describe unto us the island. And study not to be short, but declare largely in order their grounds, their rivers, their cities, their people, their manners, their ordinances, their laws, and, to be short, all things that you shall think us desirous to know." Hythlodaye agrees, but first the three men decide to dine. They return to the quiet of the garden and More gives the order to his servants "that no man should trouble us."[10] The traveller then enters into that graphic narrative comprising the second book of *Utopia,* which reflects the author's protests against the social injustices of his own time.

There can be no doubt that *Utopia* was intended for a limited audience. Following the example of Plato, More utilized dialogue in the first book. As a skilled advocate, he sought to expose the weaknesses and wrongs of that which was his target by having them defended and explained by an interlocutor. He well realized that this classic pattern of presenting his thesis could be misunderstood and misinterpreted by the untutored, and for that reason *Utopia* was not written in English. Years after its composition, in his *Confutation,* he said: "I say therefore in these days in which men by their own default misconstrue and take harm of the very scripture of God, until men better amend, if any man would now translate *Moriae* into English, or some works either that I have myself written ere this, albeit there be none harm therein, folk yet being (as they be) given to take harm of any that is good, I would, not only my darling's [meaning Erasmus] books but mine own also, help to burn them both with mine own hands, rather than folk should (though through their own fault) take any harm of them, seeing that I see them likely in these days so to do."[11]

Despite his words, misinterpretation was to linger through the centuries, until, in our own time, we find the Director of the Karl Marx-Engels Institute of the Central Executive Committee of the Union of Soviet Republics writing to the Sisters of Beaufort Street Convent in London for information "about that great communist Thomas More."

The year in which *Utopia* was published (1516) was a memorable year for Erasmian reformers as well. In February Erasmus published the greatest of his works, *Novum Instrumentum,* his Greek text of the New Testament, the editing of which had taken him sixteen years to write. A month later he published the *Institute of the Christian Prince,* dedicated to the young King, Charles of Castile and the Netherlands. It was an eloquent treatise against war and a cry for justice to the poor. In this same summer the Dutch scholar could also report that the first portion of the great edition of *Jerome* was finished and that he was dedicating it to Archbishop Warham of Canterbury. "Would that in all our princes were the same mind that is in you," he addressed the prelate, "then these insane and wretched wars would end, and rulers would turn their minds to making their age illustrious by the arts of peace."[12]

7

BEFORE *Utopia* reached the printer, Thomas Wolsey was elevated to the Cardinalate. For the reception of the Red Hat forwarded by Pope Leo, Wolsey arranged an unparalleled display to dazzle the Londoners. He despatched a Bishop and an Earl with an elaborate escort to Blackheath to meet the protonotary, bearing it to England. The Mayor and Aldermen on horseback, the City Guilds on foot, turned out to give the Hat salute as it was borne in triumph through the streets of the city to Westminster. There it reposed in state upon the high altar until the following Sunday. Three Archbishops, eight Bishops, and eight Abbots participated in the ceremonials. An eye-witness remarked that he had never seen the like, save in the coronation of a mighty prince. Dean Colet was not intimidated and preached a rousing sermon on humility. His words were unheeded. As the aged Archbishop of Canterbury, Warham, passed down the nave at the close of the ceremony, no crozier was borne before him, and none was ever again borne before him in Wolsey's presence.

A fortnight later Cardinal Wolsey urged the dissolution of Parliament. It met but once in the fourteen years that Wolsey remained in his high office. Three weeks later, on December 22, 1515, the Cardinal succeeded Warham as Lord Chancellor.

More, who had returned from his diplomatic mission to Flanders, despatched a copy of *Utopia*, fresh from the press, with a letter to Warham congratulating him upon his resignation from the heavy burden of the Chancellorship and upon the integrity with which he had borne that burden.

For the new Chancellor, More had nothing but good will. He entertained no political ambitions. Besides, the encouragement of letters furnished a strong bond between the two men. With peace at hand, the longed-for Golden Age might well return. To Erasmus he wrote: "The Archbishop has been at last relieved of the Office of Chancellor, the burden of which, as you know, he has been anxious to shake off for some years. Having secured the privacy he has long desired, he enjoys a leisure sweetened by literature, and by the recollection of important affairs well administered. The King has put in his place the Cardinal of York, who so conducts himself as to surpass the high expectation of all. After so excellent a predecessor, it is no easy matter to give, as he does, complete satisfaction."[1]

With Wolsey as Lord Chancellor, it was inevitable that More be drawn more closely into royal service. In his letter to Erasmus he expressed his distaste for ambassadorial duties. It did not suit a married man thus to leave his family, he complained; "indeed it does not seem as suitable for us laymen, as for you clergymen, who either have no wives and children, or find them wheresoever you go." This latter was a gentle jibe at his friend, himself in orders, and a significant comment on the light manner with which many of the priests of that day observed their vows.

He confessed that he had been offered a royal pension. "This, however, I have hitherto refused, and shall, I think, continue to do so, because if I took it, the place I now hold in the City, which I prefer to a higher office, would have to be given up or retained—much to my regret—and with some offence to the citizens, who, if they had any questions with the Government, as sometimes happens about their privileges, would have less confidence in me as a paid pensioner of the King.

"However, in that embassy of mine there were some very agreeable circumstances. In the first place, there was the long and constant intercourse with Tunstall, who, as he is unsurpassed in all literary accomplishments and in strictness of life and character, is at the same time a most delightful companion. Another circumstance was my acquaintance with Busleiden, who entertained me with a magnificence suitable to his noble fortune and a kindness proportioned to the goodness of his heart. He showed me a house adorned with singular taste and provided with the choicest furniture; he showed me many monuments of antiquity, of which you know I am curious, and finally his well-stored library, and a mind still better stored . . ."[2]

In February, 1516, the Queen bore Henry a child. The royal infant was a girl, who was given the name Mary.

Her godparents were Wolsey and the Duchess of Norfolk. Henry would certainly have preferred a princeling, nevertheless he displayed high spirit. A week following the birth of his daughter, he jovially confided to the Venetian Ambassador that: "We are both young; if it was a daughter this time by the grace of God the sons will follow."[3]

More might fear unhappiness in the King's service but the Cardinal was obdurate. While the royal pension dangled before More, Erasmus wrote in alarm, warning him against the atmosphere of princes and courts. More pleaded to Wolsey that he could not, in conscience, faithfully execute the duties of Under-Sheriff and at the same time receive a stipend from the King. But all his objections proved futile before the Cardinal's design, and finally, if not eagerly, he accepted the royal pension.

The year of the Princess Mary's birth was the year that Charles of Castile became King of Spain after the death of Ferdinand. The latter had died on the hunting field at the age of sixty-three. Wolsey and Henry watched sharply, waiting for the moves of his successor. Both feared France. On the great stage of European politics the interminable drama never ceased; the ordinary conflicts, the conventional treacheries, the usual game of broken treaties and expected wiles, obscuring the significance of the New Learning, all in this year that was so fruitful to the Erasmian reformers.

When Erasmus had completed his translation of the New Testament he had dedicated it to Pope Leo X and wrote gleefully to More that it was approved by those "whom I thought most likely to find fault; and the leading theologians like it very much."[4] It was a work of high importance, and quite naturally there were critics aplenty to

look askance at what they considered a challenge to tradition. His friend, Martin Dorp, canon and theologian of
Louvain, had earlier sent a message of apprehension to the
master: "This is another matter upon which in all friendship I have longed to convey a warning to a friend . . . You
are proposing to correct the Latin copies by the Greek. But
if I show that the Latin version has no mixture of falsehood
or mistake, will you not admit that such a work is unneces-
sary? But this is what I claim for the Vulgate, since it is
unreasonable to suppose that the Universal Church has
been in error for so many generations in her use of this
edition, nor is it probable that so many holy Fathers have
been mistaken, who in reliance upon it have defined the
most arduous questions in General Councils, which, it is
admitted by most theologians as well as lawyers, are not
subject to error in matters of faith."[5]

Erasmus made ready reply to this letter, but More offered an abler defence: "Erasmus is not as you seem to
suppose a mere grammarian but a theologian too, and he
is only at pains to criticize those who give themselves up to
scholastic subtleties—men as far removed from true theology as they are from common sense . . ."[6] In a long letter
to Dorp he stressed that Scriptural studies must not be
sacrificed to scholastic theology: ". . . I cannot hear it said
that these minute questionings are more useful than the
knowledge of the sacred writings to the flock for which
Christ died. If you merely contend that these things are
worth studying, I will not contest it; but if you put them
on a level with the dissertations of the ancient Fathers, I
cannot listen to you.

"I do not think you will contest this with me, that whatever is necessary for salvation is communicated to us in the first place from the Sacred Scriptures, then from the ancient interpreters, and by traditional customs handed down through the ancient Fathers from hand to hand, and, finally, by the sacred definitions of the Church. If, in addition to all this, these acute disputants have curiously discovered anything, though I grant it may be convenient and useful, yet I think it belongs to the class of things without which it is possible to live . . . The reason why the ancient interpreters are so much neglected is because certain unhappy geniuses have first persuaded themselves, and then led others to believe, that there is nowhere any honey besides what has already been stored in the hives of the Summists . . ."[7]

With such encouragement from More, Erasmus was spurred on, and now finally the great work, after sixteen years of prodigious toil, was finished, and the happy author wrote: "I would have the weakest woman read the Gospels and the Epistles of St. Paul . . . I would have those words translated into all languages, so that not only Scots and Irish, but Turks and Saracens too might read them. I long for the ploughboy to sing them to himself as he follows the plough, the weaver to hum them to the tune of his shuttle, the traveller to beguile with them the dullness of his journey . . . Other studies we may regret to have undertaken, but happy is the man upon whom death comes when he is engaged in these. These sacred words give you the very image of Christ speaking, healing, dying, rising again, and make him so present, that were he before your very eyes you would not more truly see him."[8]

More was giving service to the King, but as yet he had

not been persuaded or pressed into permanent employ. He still practiced law and still occupied his beloved office of Under-Sheriff. But there now came two incidents which would strengthen Wolsey's resolve into a command. A law suit existed between the Royal and Papal states in the matter of a Papal vessel which, it was charged, had illegally put into the port of Southampton and had thus violated the law of the nations. The Crown had seized the ship and claimed her as a forfeit. More was retained by the Nuncio, and the trial was eventually relayed to the Star Chamber. It was an event complete with the solemn paraphernalia and persons of the Chief Justices, the Lord Treasurer, and the magnificence of the Lord Chancellor himself. Even the King attended. But More was neither intimidated nor bewildered by his audience. He argued with his usual brilliance and logic, and the judgment was delivered in his favour. Both King and Cardinal listened to his arguments with keen appreciation, both all the more convinced that they were witness to a talent which must be diverted to their use and to their ends.

Then came "Evil May Day," long to be a black memory in London. Once again the measure of More was displayed, although in a different way. May Day was a traditional day of play for all Englishmen, and for the multitude of London 'prentices it was the great occasion for undisciplined fun and demonstration. In 1517, their mood was ugly. The twisted streets of the capital hummed with the business of many crafts and trades: haberdashers, weavers, cappers, tailors, butchers, grocers, vintners, waterbearers, candlemakers, chandlers, brewers, fellmongers, saddlers, leathersellers, blacksmiths, goldsmiths, armourers, swordmakers, vendors of all kind and description. It was only natural that the rich markets should attract merchants and skilled artificers from abroad. There were nearly five thousand Flemish weavers living in the city, and there was also a flourishing colony of Frenchmen. Italians lent money, carved stone, and made fine furniture. The Hanseatic merchants of the Steelyard, "a walled German community in the very midst of London," brought in and sold timber, tar, rope, iron, and wax. And as the babble of alien tongues increased, so too did the resentment of the Londoners. During Easter week a popular priest spoke against the foreigners: "The aliens and strangers," he cried from the pulpit, "eat the bread from the poor fatherless children, and take the living from all the artificers, and the intercourse from all the merchants, whereby poverty is so much increased that every man bewails the misery of others, for craftsmen be brought to beggary and merchants to neediness."[9]

The talk went fast and hot. A Frenchman had abducted and, it was said, maltreated an Englishman's wife. Furthermore, he boasted of it, and one of his fellow countrymen said loudly that if he had the Mayor's wife of London they would keep her. A sturdy mercer by name of William Bolt gave angry reply: "Well, you whoreson Lombards, you rejoice and laugh, by the Mass we will one day have a day at you, come when it will."[10] Rumours and tales circulated like fever, becoming all the wilder in passing from mouth to mouth. London was ready for riot and bloodshed.

On the Eve of May Day, the City sent for two officials, More and the City Recorder, Richard Brook, to receive instructions from the Cardinal. They returned to the Guildhall with a peremptory instruction that a curfew be imposed that very night on all citizens, their 'prentices and servants. It was an impracticable and unpopular command, and when one rash alderman attempted to enforce it, a mob sprang into being. The rallying cry of "Clubs and Prentices" quickly brought hordes of excited and resentful recruits from doorways and corners. Mischief grew to violence, a prison was breached, and while terrified foreigners hid, there was sacking and burning. The alarmed Wolsey sent for the Earl of Surrey, who immediately set out for the city with a sizeable force of armed men. Sir Richard Cholmeley, Lieutenant of the Tower, manned and exploded his clumsy cannon, making a great noise but doing little damage.

While Surrey's men were converging, it was More who ventured out into the darkness and faced the rabble, parleying and reasoning, meeting fury with common sense. There was much stone-throwing and shouting of threats, but the Under-Sheriff stood his ground with calmness and courage. Later in the century it was surely Shakespeare who was to exalt this moment in the play, *Sir Thomas More*.

When the rioters demanded that all aliens be removed from London, the playwright has More answer:

> *Grant them removed, and grant that this your noise*
> *Hath chid down all the majesty of England.*
> *Imagine that you see the wretched strangers,*
> *Their babies at their backs, and their poor luggage,*
> *Plodding to the ports and coasts for transportation,*
> *And that you sit as kings in your desires,*
> *Authority quite silenced by your brawl,*

And you in ruff of your opinion clothed,
What had you got? I'll tell you. You had taught
How insolence and strong hand should prevail,
How order should be quelled; and by this pattern
Not one of you should live an aged man;
For other ruffians, as their fancies wrought
With self same hand, self reasons and self right
Would shark on you; and men like ravenous fishes
Would feed on one another.[11]

Most of the rioters dispersed during the early morning hours, and soon the City officials, aided by sundry noblemen and their armed retainers, succeeded in restoring complete order. And now Henry, who had been safe at Richmond, gave early demonstration of that cruel tyranny which later was to mark his every act. The street rioting, because of the King's friendship with foreign nations, was considered to be treason, and the punishments to be so measured. Gallows were hastily thrown up around the city. Thirteen unfortunate wretches were summarily hanged, then drawn and quartered. Others were held for the same treatment. Shocked by this harshness, the Mayor and Aldermen met and appointed a deputation to wait on the King and to beg for leniency. More led the group to the Royal presence. Dressed in black they made the appeal, but were coldly told to address their plea to the Lord Chancellor. Wolsey had little liking for blood, but knowing his master, and with his genius for high ceremony and pageant, he proceeded to put on a great spectacle. The King in solemn state, accompanied by his Queen and Court, came to Westminster Hall. The chosen prisoners, four hundred men and boys and eleven women, were mustered before his cold stare, and each one stripped for the gibbet, a halter around each neck. Kneeling before the monarch, they begged for mercy. The King refused to be moved. The Queen fell to her knees and added her voice and tears. The Lords Spiritual and Temporal joined in the appeal. Henry refused again, but finally after another speech from Wolsey he magnanimously granted the pardon. There were wild shouts of rejoicing and gratitude. Standing there witness to it all, indeed a first actor in the scene, dressed in his mourning black, was the author of *Utopia*. A thunder of voices was raised for the King, but in many hearts the real salute was given to Lawyer More. He, more than anyone, had stayed the riot before it grew to rebellion. And he, as Wolsey was well aware, had played a major part in dissipating the Royal vengeance. Henceforth there could be no alternative. All the hours of this wise man, this respected man, this good man, must be given the King.

More's Humanist friends were sorry to see him enter the Royal service, but at least his wife was happy. She had long considered it foolish for him to reject Wolsey's overtures. And once she had chided him for not being sufficiently ambitious. "Will you sit still by the fire and make goslings in the ashes with a stick as children do? . . . for as my mother was wont to say . . . it is ever better to rule than to be ruled."

"By my truth, wife," answered More, "in this I dare say you say truth, for I never found you willing to be ruled yet."[12]

There were many duties awaiting the King's new servant. In August, More was commissioned to travel across the

Channel again, this time to stay in Calais and negotiate a
trading pact with the French merchants. Before he sailed
there was another emergency in London. A plague-like
disease, the dreaded "Sweating Sickness," swept the city
and its environs, bringing horror and death and much confusion. The King moved to a remote place in the country,
but not before many close to him, including his pages and
one of his secretaries, had died. The disease, probably born
of the filth of the congested and ill-kept streets, was enor-
mously potent, killing off its victims within the first twenty-
four hours. Nor was it a respecter of rank. The Cardinal
was stricken three times and barely survived. The deathcart
was as familiar to the doors of the noble household as it was
to the darkest corner of some lowly lane. More helped keep
order in the city and later was given the task of improving
conditions at Oxford, where the plague had also struck.
He saw to it that some measures of quarantine were undertaken; infected houses were given markings, and those
good people who visited and nursed the victims were instructed to carry white wands.

"Deaths are frequent all around us," he wrote to Erasmus, "almost everybody at Oxford, at Cambridge, and here
in London, having been laid up within the last few days,
and very many of our best and most honoured friends being
lost . . . For in this Sweating Sickness, as they call it, no one
dies but on the first day. I, with my wife and children, am
as yet untouched; the rest of my family have recovered. I
can assure you that there is less danger up on a field of
battle, than in this town. It is now, I hear, beginning
to rage at Calais, when we are being forced thither ourselves to undertake a diplomatic mission—as if it were not

enough to have been living in contagion here without following it elsewhere. But what is one to do? What our lot
brings us must be borne; and I have composed my mind
for every event."[13]

The stay at Calais with its dull business of bickering and
compromise, the long absence from his home, was a sacrifice for the man who was so much the good parent and
complete Londoner. Erasmus informed him that he had
been offered a commission by the Emperor, but that he
should do anything "rather than become entangled in that
kind of business; and how glad I should be if you were
clear."[14] More replied: "I approve of your plan in not wish-
ing to be involved in the busy trifles of Princes; and you
show your love for me by desiring that I may be disen-
tangled from such matters, in which you can scarcely
believe how unwillingly I am engaged. Nothing indeed can
be more hateful to me than my present mission. I am sent to
stay at a little seaport, with a disagreeable soil and climate;
and whereas at home I have naturally the greatest abhor-
rence of litigation, even when it brings me profit, you may
imagine what annoyance it must cause one here, when it
comes accompanied with loss."[15]

As a relief to the "litigation" More kept his pen busy.
There was certainly much to discuss with his Humanist
friends; Erasmus' great triumph with the New Testament;
his own success with *Utopia;* the hope springing from papal
efforts to achieve a universal peace amongst the Christian
nations. For in the August of 1517, Leo X, fearing the
Turk, had promulgated a Bull which sought to impose a five
years' truce on the Princes of Europe. Then there were the
high maneuverings of Wolsey, whose "balance of power"

policy, ostensibly to protect the Papacy but certainly not harmful to England's interest, prompted Henry to subsidize the young scion of the Hapsburgs, Charles of Castile, soon to be Emperor. This youth, already occupant of his father's dukedom of Burgundy, was now ready for his Spanish inheritance. A loan was arranged, and off sailed the grandson of Ferdinand and Isabella to occupy his kingdom. And then there were all the signs of the great storm that was gathering over Germany. Luther did not nail his "Ninety-five Theses" to the door of Wittenberg Cathedral until the November of this year. But Tetzel, the Dominican orator and fund raiser, had, by means of his vigorous money-gathering campaign and improper traffic in Indulgences, made an opportune scandal that was to prove ready and valuable ammunition for those who were to reject the papal supremacy.

8

NEITHER royal service nor the traffic of many guests prevented More from supervising in detail the training of his children. The household was a testing ground for his theories of education. Here was taught and lived the Christian belief that in a perfect society there would be two authorities, the natural and the supernatural, and that the latter, being God's will, should govern the first. This is what he taught in his home; it was the rule by which he lived; it was the principle for which he died.

He did not send his children to school, for he had his own ideas as to their training. The best of tutors were brought in, and they lived as members of the family. The excellent school, St. Paul's, which had been founded by his friend Colet, was not far away, yet his son John was kept and educated at home. In an age when the education of females was mostly confined to domestic virtues, his daughters, Margaret, Elizabeth, Cecily, and his adopted daughter, Margaret Giggs, were given a thorough grounding, along with their brother, in Latin, Greek, Logic, Philosophy, Theology, Mathematics, and even Astronomy. To teach the latter subject came Master Nicholas Kratzer, German-born and formerly a fellow of Corpus, Oxford. Serving with him were also Master Drew, Richard Hyrde, and William Gunnell. When More was forced by his official duties to journey abroad or attend the Court, he kept supervision over his family's training by letters both to the tutors and to the children.

To Gunnell came an admonition on the necessity of humility and the danger of pride: ". . . the more I see the difficulty of getting rid of this pest of pride, the more do I see the necessity of setting to work at it from childhood. For I find no other reason why this evil clings so to our hearts, than because almost as soon as we are born, it is sown in the tender minds of children by their nurses, it is cultivated by their teachers, and brought to its full growth by their parents; no one teaching even what is good without, at the same time, awakening the expectation of praise, as of the proper reward of virtue. Thus we grow accustomed to make so much of praise, that while we study how to please the greater number (who will always be the worst), we grow ashamed of being good (with the few). That this plague of vainglory may be banished far from my children, I do desire that you, my dear Gunnell, and their mother and all their friends, would sing this song to them, and repeat it, and beat it into their heads, that vainglory is a thing despicable, and to be spit upon; and that there is nothing more sublime than that humble modesty so often praised by Christ; and this your prudent charity will so enforce as to teach virtue rather than reprove vice, and make them love good advice instead of hating it. . . If you will teach something of this sort . . . you will bind me and them still more to you. And thus you will bring about that my children, who are dear to me by nature, and still more dear by learning and virtue, will become most dear by that advance in knowledge and good conduct."[1]

More's daughters and son were not the only ones to be educated in his house. There was his step-daughter and his wards, there was his daughters' maid, Dorothy Colley, there were other servants, and his official duties grew along with a resultant enlargement of staff. Various secretaries and pages imbibed the training and spirit of this unique school. His eldest daughter seems to have been the prize pupil, and More justifiably took great pride in her very considerable scholarship. She became fluent in Greek and Latin and earned the respect of More's friends. Erasmus wrote to her as an equal and referred to her as "Britanica's Jewel." Cardinal Pole professed his astonishment at her learning. The Bishop of Exeter saluted her with a gold coin.

In the summer of 1521 Margaret married William Roper. Her husband was a young lawyer who already had been given the hospitality of More's roof. More, as the old saying goes, "did not lose a daughter but gained a son." Margaret and her husband continued to live with him, and in doing so set a pattern that was followed by his other children and wards in their turn.

His good wife, Dame Alice, "of good years, and of no favour or complexion," tried valiantly to follow the conver-

sation of her husband's guests and the equally high talk
of the children's learning. Although it was mostly over her
head, she understood the aims of More's programme. Not
meant to be a student herself, she adopted the role of a
stern headmistress and supplied her own lack by keeping
a watchful eye on the children. Hours of study were rigidly
enforced and there was little malingering or evasion under
the rule of Dame Alice.

The pursuit of secular learning, arduous though it might
seem, was not made at the expense of religion. Worship of
God was the predominant thought and practice of the little
community; piety was the order of every day and family
prayers were recited morning and evening. Mass was attended daily and excerpts from the Scriptures were read
at mealtime. The great feasts of the Church were carefully
explained and solemnly observed. With the discipline he
had acquired from the Carthusians, More usually left his
bed before two in the morning and from then until seven
spent the hours in prayer or religious reading. He taught
the family the necessity and nobility of charity by practical
examples. He welcomed poor and rich alike to his house.
He built an alms-house which was cared for by the entire
family. With so many things to do, More would yet find
time to pay calls on less fortunate neighbours, "helping
them not with small gifts but with two, three, or four pieces
of gold, as their need required."[2] He saved no money: all
went to his house and his charities.

Despite the stress on religion and learning, More's house
was not a gloomy one. There was much fun and play. Dice
and gambling were forbidden but there were other games
and play-acting to lighten the hours. Everyone, including

HENRY VIII

the servants, was encouraged to play a musical instrument of some kind. Even Dame Alice, severe and stiff on occasion, yielded to the lure of music and, practicing daily, achieved some success with the lute, the viol, the monochord and the flute. More enjoyed a good joke and, as his station advanced and as was the custom then, he kept a jester, one Patenson, in residence. More had a pet monkey, the source of much mischief and amusement, and being fond of animals he made a collection of sizeable proportions which inhabited his gardens. Said Erasmus: "One of his amusements is in observing the forms, characters and instincts of different animals. Accordingly there is scarcely any kind of bird that he does not keep about his residence, and the same of other animals not quite so common, as monkeys, foxes, ferrets, weasels, and the like. Besides these, if he meets with any strange object, imported from abroad . . . he is most eager to buy it . . . and his own pleasure is renewed every time that he sees others interested."[3]

His domestic life with all its numerous interests and enjoyments was punctuated by absences when he was obliged to wait upon the King and attend the Court. Henry took great pride in his acquisition of More and insisted that his new servant be in constant and close personal attendance. This caused considerable hardship to More, who, in addition to missing his family, had all the philosopher's distaste for the life of a courtier. To make everything all the more difficult there was a series of new and violent outbreaks of the Sweating Sickness. To avoid the dread disease Henry constantly moved his residence. In 1518, More's first year of complete royal service, the King shifted his Court no fewer than six times.

When pressure had first been applied upon More to enter the King's service he had realized that to do so would mean that he would no longer be able to serve the City as Under-Sheriff. Nevertheless, he did not resign this office that he liked so much until some time after he had been officially appointed as a King's Councillor and made Master of Requests.

In spite of his many activities he yet found time to make a spirited defence of the teaching of Greek at Oxford. And this was no ordinary court of an ordinary prince that he had come to attend. This was the court of the brilliant and enlightened young Henry, still the hope of scholars and reformers. "I should deplore the fortune of More in being enticed into a Court," wrote Erasmus to Tunstall, "if it were not that under such a King, and with so many learned men for companions and colleagues, it may seem not a Court, but a temple of the Muses."[4] More expressed the same optimism when he wrote to his friend John Fisher still at Cambridge: "It was with the greatest unwillingness that I came to Court, as everyone knows, and as the King himself in joke often throws up in my face. I am as uncomfortable there as a bad rider is in the saddle. I am far from enjoying the special favour of the King, but he is so courteous and kindly to all that everyone who is in any way hopeful finds a ground for imagining that he is in the King's good graces. . . But I am not so happy as to perceive signs of favour or so hopeful as to imagine them. But the King has virtue and learning, and makes great progress in both, with daily renewed zeal, so that the more I see His Majesty advance in all the qualities that befit a good monarch, the less burdensome do I feel this life of the Court."[5]

The tragic hour was to come when More was to utter the historic words that he died, "the King's good servant, but God's first." Surely then his memory reached back to this first year of his royal service, when Henry had greeted him with a pious warning, "that in all his doings and affairs touching the King, he should first respect and regard God, and afterward the King his master."[6]

High ideals and great deeds of goodness had not yet left Henry's horizon. He was greatly pleased that he could now, in his own household and at any time, command More's conversation. It was noted that the king's custom was, "upon holidays, when he had done his own devotions, to send for him into his travers, and there, sometime in matters of Astronomy, Geometry, Divinity, and such other Faculties, and sometimes of his worldly affairs, to sit and confer with him. And other whiles would he, in the night, have him up into his leads, there for to consider with him the diversities, courses, motions and operations of the stars and planets. And, because he was of a pleasant disposition, it pleased the King and Queen, after the Council had supped . . . commonly to call for him to be merry with them."[7]

This popularity with the King was all very well, but for a man so devoted to his own hearth, it was also irksome. There were times when his liberty from the Court did not exceed two days a month. Realizing the error of being too entertaining a courtier, he sought to employ a different tactic. ". . . much misliking this restraint of his liberty, began thereupon somewhat to dissemble his nature, and so by little and little from his former accustomed mirth to disuse himself, that he was of them from thenceforth at such seasons no more so ordinarily sent for."[8] In other words, he pretended to be dull, but the ruse never fully succeeded.

If it were certain that More should eventually run afoul of his patron, Henry, it was equally sure that, sooner or later, his course would run counter to that of Wolsey, no less his sponsor. The prelate was now nearing the height of his power, living with a magnificence that even surpassed the splendour of the King's court. He received homage and bribes at home and from abroad. Noblemen and prelates of all ranks attended his person. He was only in his middle forties and he had been humbly born, yet when the King's Arms were put up, his appeared alongside of them. Money was minted, bearing his Cardinal's Hat. Oxford addressed him as "Your Majesty." Each year he accumulated more and richer benefices. A great army of retainers, knights, squires, chamberlains, priests, yeomen, grooms, pages, crowded his vast household. His master cook paraded in damask and velvet with a chain of gold about his neck. When Wolsey travelled it was always in state. Swelling the procession were his private heralds and physicians and apothecaries and minstrels. He was Lord Chancellor of England, Cardinal of the Holy Roman Church, and now, at this time, *Legate a latere,* possessing the plenary power of the Pope in England, the right to exercise supreme ecclesiastical authority, a distinction which he valued more than the Great Seal itself. There had never been anyone like him in England before (nor, for that matter, has there been since). There seemed to be no end to his avarice or demands for more authority. His belief in his own greatness was equally boundless. He possessed a mistress, and her brother was his confessor. His predecessor in the Chancellorship, Archbishop Warham cried: "Know ye not that this man is drunk with too much prosperity?" The voice of the aged prelate was unheeded, for Wolsey's greatness and genius could not be over-ridden. England's star was in the ascendant, and it was he who directed the power of the Crown. His hand was felt in all activities, good or bad. Irregular though his own conduct might be, he sought to correct many a clerical abuse, and in his grand manner was a patron of the universities.

As Lord Chancellor, the Cardinal proceeded from York House to Westminster Hall with pomp and pageantry. And there, forced to participate in the glitter by his duties, was Thomas More. One wonders what his thoughts were when he heard the heralds blare, followed by the loud cry: "On, my Lords and Masters, on before; make way for my Lord's Grace." Wolsey in his sumptuous robes of scarlet brocade, gold-slippered, sat on a golden cushion, a long procession preceding his person, bearing the symbols of his authority, the Great Seal of England, the Cardinal's Hat, the two great silver crosses which testified to his possession of York and the Legatine power, two tall pillars of silver, and finally his pursuivant at arms, in elaborate livery, carrying the great mace of silver gilt. It was a common joke that "the two crosses showed that the Cardinal had twice as many sins to repent of as any other prelate."

The contrast was great indeed between the Lord Chancellor and the man who was to succeed him in that office—Thomas More in as simple a garb as could be allowed and hidden beneath the plain coat always the penance of the hair shirt. For Wolsey saw to it that the new councillor played an important part in his ceremonies.

When the famed canonist, Cardinal Campeggio, visited England that summer a dazzling welcome of gigantic proportions was staged. The Italian had been sent by Leo X to seek English support for his dream of a great and united crusade. But he had not been allowed to land in England until the Pope had first met Wolsey's terms. Campeggio cooled his heels at Calais while Wolsey demanded, and received, the Bull that made him *Legate a latere* and thus assured him precedence. Along with the Bull he also demanded the revenues of the rich bishopric of Bath and Wells. The Pope yielded, Campeggio crossed the Channel, whereupon Wolsey sought to impress him with English hospitality. He was met by the Bishop of Chichester and the Lords of Kent. A large troop of knights brought him to Sandwich, where he stayed the night. Next morning a greater cavalcade took him to Canterbury, where he was received by the Archbishop, the Bishop of Rochester, the Abbots of St. Augustine and Faversham, the Priors of Christ Church and St. Gregory. A mighty choir of monks chanted while he knelt before St. Thomas' shrine. The way to London was studded with ceremonies, banquets and speeches. At Blackheath the Duke of Norfolk met him with two thousand horse.

Before he entered London proper he was taken to a tent of gold where he was changed to richer robes. The long procession formed, the silver cross went forward. The clergy of the city met him vested in copes of gold and swinging their censers, and around them the crowds alternately gaped and cheered at the spectacle. At London bridge the procession halted for the official greeting by the Guilds, the Mayor, the Aldermen in their best liveries, the canons of

St. Paul's, and the Bishop of London. Thomas More had been chosen to speak for the city. He spoke in Latin, but realizing the length of the ceremonies that had gone before and with the knowledge that there was still much more to come, he considerately made his oration brief, thereby undoubtedly pleasing the highly impressed but weary Italians.

Campeggio's proposal for a united Christendom met with no opposition from Wolsey. A united Christendom offered play for his imagination. There was, as the Pope desperately cried, a dire need for unity. The new Sultan of the Turks, Selim the Grim, had conquered Syria and Egypt and had extended his boundaries in the East. Having mustered his fierce armies with determination and skill, he threatened Belgrade, the key to Hungary, and at the same time his corsairs made forays into Rhodes, bastion of the Mediterranean. Once these two outposts of Christendom were taken it would not be difficult for the warriors of Islam to wreak all the terrors of a Holy War upon a disunited Italy and a supine Germany.

The Pope's Legates appealed to the Christian nations to unite against the invaders. In England, although far from the menace of the Scimitar, both Wolsey and Henry listened with sympathy, and with excitement. A united Christendom required a leader. There was the Pope, of course, but the temporal power of the Papal States was as nothing. A pope who would be grateful to a protector, a pope intimidated, a pope who took advice from Machiavelli, a pope who was one of the Medici clan could be controlled. And he was but mortal, a fact which surely whirled in Wolsey's fertile brain. The conclave who chose the next pope would be dominated by that strong Prince who was the champion of all Christians, who would bring substance to the idea that was the Holy Roman Empire. The present wearer of the shadowy crown was Maximilian, whose heir was Charles of Castile, the same who had gone to Spain with Henry's assistance. The unreal office of the Emperor, so sought by all the princes, was not hereditary but elective. If France and Spain could be kept in balance, if the Seven Electors could be managed, it was an intoxicating prospect for such as Wolsey, confident in his own genius, unbridled in his lust for power, sure that the direction and favour of his royal master would ever be his.

A pact was quickly drafted and given shape. France and England agreed to a permanent peace and promised mutual aid in the event of attack from the east. All the greater sovereign powers and princes were invited to join and share the responsibilities of the alliance. War within Christendom was at last to be outlawed, and all problems and grievances were to be settled by arbitration instead of bloodshed. It was a mirage, but it was a glorious mirage. There was a great scurry of ambassadors and agents, but the indomitable Wolsey held the reins, and the whip too, and apparently overcame all obstacles. The needed seals and signatures were obtained, and at St. Paul's the Treaty of London was ratified with every solemnity. It had been the Pope's idea, but Wolsey had seized the initiative. His King's name graced the head and foot of the document. His own signature was at the bottom, along with those of Norfolk and Suffolk. In this exalted company was Thomas More. It was on the second day of October in 1518 that the large hope was pledged. The universal peace that was to last for-

ver did in fact exist for thirty agitated months and was
hen followed by thirty years of a vicious and terrible con-
lict which tore all Europe asunder.

The Venetian Ambassador to Henry at that time was
Sebastian Giustinian. He was a shrewd man and a keen
observer, and from his report we learn of the growing importance of More at Court, also something of his discretion
and close-lipped common sense. While the negotiations
were proceeding between England and France, Giustinian,
conscientious diplomat that he was, sought to know everything there was to be known concerning the projected alliance. After an unsatisfactory conversation with Henry he
made it his business to engage with More. "I adroitly turned
the conversation on these negotiations concerning peace;
but he did not open and pretended not to know in what the
difficulties consisted, declaring that the Cardinal of York
most solely'. . . transacted the matter with French ambassadors, and, when he was concluded, he then calls the
councillors, so that the King himself scarcely knows in what
state matters are."[9] More added that the Spanish ambassador had likewise received no information respecting these
matters, except the assurance that nothing would be introduced in the negotiations at variance with the amity existing
between England and his sovereign.

More's signature was affixed to another important document at this time, the betrothal of little Princess Mary and
the son of the French King. For Wolsey, in his high game,
thus sought by blood ties to secure the new friendship between France and England. It was a move that could bring
no pleasure in Spain, nor to Mary's mother, but in the
interests of the promised peace Catherine quelled her Span-

ish sympathies and submissively presented her daughter to
the French envoys.

As a Humanist More could dream of peace, but as a
realist he could only despair as he witnessed the Cardinal's
trafficking. His opportunities for observation became the
greater as he was called upon to play an increasingly important role in England's affairs. Very little time elapsed
before the Treaty of London met its first test.

The Emperor Maximilian suddenly died and the coveted
title became vacant. The three important candidates were
Francis, King of France and Duke of Milan, Charles, King
of Spain, possessor of South Italy, of the Netherlands, and
now the Hapsburg lands, and Henry, King of England. On
the Continent, as the agents sped amongst the Electors bar-
gaining and bribing, there was little serious consideration
given to Henry's cause. The votes were cast and soon at
Frankfort the heralds proclaimed that Charles of Spain
was to be Holy Roman Emperor. Wolsey had lost his
gamble, yet England's power became all the more important in the struggle that was looming between France and
Spain, and both Francis and Charles were quick to bid for
Henry's favour.

It was arranged that the English King should visit
France, but before this could happen Charles announced
that he would come to England. All this business required
complicated negotiation, and to More were entrusted many
of the details. It required constant association with Henry
who was ever delighted with the wit and wisdom of his
unassuming courtier. The liking became a friendship, and
while More became the more intimate with his sovereign
Wolsey was becoming more isolated in his own grandeur

The Cardinal had not won the Imperial Crown for Henry, but with the Kings of Spain and France courting his influence, he had not abandoned yet his own hopes for the tiara. He worked for England, but in the press of his activities, both at home and abroad, he was underestimating the capacities of Henry. Neglected even were the forms of protocol when dealing with the foreign princes, and often and publicly in matters of important decision he dispensed with the formal phraseology of speaking as the King's representative.

Charles landed in England a bare five days before Henry departed for France. He received a suitably warm welcome, particularly from the Queen, his aunt. She naturally had a poor opinion of the alliance with France, and, for that matter, so did most of Henry's subjects, for France was the traditional enemy. Henry took Charles to Canterbury. They prayed and talked together; the pale young Hapsburg and the jovial, full-blooded Henry, now twenty-nine years old. It is sure that, under the direction of the Cardinal, no commitments were made, but there were many assurances, and Charles had to be content with these. Thomas More was in the fringe of all this, being both councillor and royal secretary. And with distaste he learned that it was expected he should accompany the court to France. Emperor and King went to their ships on the same morning. The banner of St. George unfurled to the same breeze that fluttered the black double-eagle on its golden ground. The cannons boomed their salutes. Henry's captains set course for Calais. The Spanish fleet made for the Netherlands.

The meeting between Henry and Francis provided Wolsey with the opportunity of creating one of his most costly pageants. An army of craftsmen preceded the royal party across the Channel and erected a camp that in verity was a small town; the Cardinal was determined that the spectacle should be of a magnitude and sumptuousness that would never be forgotten. The rendezvous on the field of the Cloth of Gold would display England's splendour and power to all Europe. Three thousand tents and pavilions housed Henry's entourage. Twelve golden apostles graced the royal chapel and thirty-five chaplains kept it served. A staff of two hundred cooks, scullions and attendants thronged the King's kitchen, and wine splashed and flowed continuously in his courtyard fountain. The Cardinal ceremoniously opened the twenty-five day festival by riding to the French camp in a gorgeous procession. Fifty of his gentlemen attendants rode first, wearing scarlet velvet and golden chains, then fifty of his gentlemen ushers, bareheaded, preceded the rich symbols of all his ranks, temporal and spiritual. The gold maces were as "large as a man's head at one end." There were noblemen superbly mounted and suitably escorted with horses richly caparisoned. A hundred archers marched shoulder-to-shoulder. The Cardinal wore his Red Hat with its long silken tassels, and a fine linen rochet offset the scarlet of his velvet gown. The same bright velvet provided the wrappings for his mule, and the stirrups and buckles and harness which further ornamented that animal were made of fine gold.

Great guns of bronze thundered a welcome to the French king. Francis was escorted by the Grand Constable of France. Henry, a shining figure in silver damask, was flanked by his Grand Constable, the Duke of Buckingham, already disliked by Wolsey and soon to lose his head.

Each hour of each day was part of an elaborate schedule designed by the Cardinal to stress the friendship that had been pledged between the two nations. Solemn High Masses were offered. There were innumerable feasts and jousting and games of all kinds. The Kings tried to outdo each other in manifestations of cordiality and hospitality. The Spanish-born Catherine gave the kiss of peace to the French Queen. But throughout the riot of splendour and ceremony there was the strain of falsehood. The stress was shown once when, in an exuberant mood at the games, Henry made a hold on Francis and shouted a challenge to wrestle. There was a grapple and a throw, and it was Henry who was tossed to the ground. He took it ill, England's honour had been impugned. Rising slowly to his feet, he muttered fiercely that he would on with the fight. Anxious courtiers were quick to their duty, and led away the truculent prince.

The festivities went on, but the waste of money and effort achieved little and deceived nobody. Francis, no matter what the English might do, had made up his mind to attack the Emperor before the latter could forge his disorganized inheritance into a dangerous unity. And Henry, to the delight of his Spanish-born Queen, already had arranged another meeting with the Emperor. Wolsey might wish to deal with the French King, but most Englishmen felt relief when the tents were struck and the exit made. "When I meet these Frenchmen again," shouted one English gentleman, "I hope it may with my sword point!"

The Emperor waited patiently at Gravelines and the double game went on. The assurances that had been given him at Canterbury were endorsed, and at the same time messengers sped back to Francis, also bearing promises.

It was delicate play and the stakes were high. Trade with Spain must not be jeopardized, but there was commerce with France too. Wolsey pondered, accepting gold from both sides, not forgetting either that the Pope was ailing, and at the next conclave both Charles and Francis would each control a sizeable number of votes.

In the Emperor's party was Erasmus, and at Calais he met with More, bringing with him a friend who was a noted Greek scholar and an official at the Spanish court. The Humanists were ever a tonic to each other, and after the colossal hypocrisies, vanities and useless extravagances of the Field of the Cloth of Gold, the conversation of intellectual peers was a joy to More.

A rush of talk followed the first salute. Each had much to tell and report, much to deplore, some things to hope for, and, to leaven the more serious themes, there was that exercise of agile wit which leaped into being whenever the two men were brought together.

9

IN the spring of 1521, Henry conferred knighthood upon
More. At the same time he was appointed Sub-Treas-
urer of the Exchequer, a post that carried more
dignity and a much larger salary. Not long after, another
recipient of the King's favour also received further preferment: Sir Thomas Boleyn was made Treasurer of the
Royal Household. By now the Boleyns were firmly en-
trenched at Court, and Mary, the sister of young Anne,
was the present target of the King's fancy; for by this time,
Henry made no pretence of fidelity to his sombre Queen.
A succession of dalliances, mixed with the pleasures of the
chase and joust, lightened and was in constant contrast to
the more serious obligations of the crown. Already the
King had achieved extra-maritally what had been denied
him in matrimony. He had sired a son by one of his wife's

maids-in-waiting, Elizabeth Blount. The child was called Henry Fitzroy, and later created the Duke of Richmond.

In May More was knighted, and it was in this same month that Wolsey saw fit to take official notice of the peril that was emanating from Germany. He commanded that the books of Martin Luther be burned in St. Paul's churchyard. A throne was built so that the Cardinal, both as Lord Chancellor and as Legate, could preside over England's gesture towards those who sought to destroy the established order. Flanking him in person and sentiment were the great people of the court and of the Church and the City.

That it would take more than ceremonial flames to quench a far greater conflagration was a thought that did not seem to disturb the Cardinal's busy mind. With all his genius for the wide scan, with all his capacity for analysis and action, with all his machinery of agents and information, Cardinal Wolsey did not grasp the full significance of what was happening in Germany. He did not foresee the terrible tearing of the fabric of Christendom. He, whose eyes were fixed on Rome, who thought himself to be so much a strength to the papacy, did not realize the speed with which the infection would take hold in England. He could not know, as he sat there watching the flames devour Luther's books, that in a future day a blame would be placed on him for the terrible schism that was to come. As Legate and Lord Chancellor he demonstrated to his King that the authority and rule of Church and State could be vested in one person. Little did this priest who wielded the secular power, this Englishman who had demanded the Legatine authority, realize that his arbitrary rule, his haughty dictatorship, would spawn that terrible legacy of anti-clerical and anti-papal feeling which has persisted in England to this day.

Bishop Fisher of Rochester had been chosen to preach when Luther's books were given to the flames, and the King thought so much of the sermon that he ordered it translated into Latin, and preserved. Henry fancied himself as a theologian. In an effort to display his talents in this science as well as to show his devotion to the Holy See, he embarked upon the composition of his famous *Assertion of the Seven Sacraments*. It was written in Latin, and the royal author sought the advice and assistance of some of his more eminent scholars, including More and Fisher. More seems to have acted in the capacity of editor, for he later declared that he was only "a sorter out and placer of the principal matters therein contained."

With the clear perception of his legal mind he saw a danger in the King's extravagant prose. The Pope's spiritual authority should be defended, but Leo X also possessed all the troubles and weaknesses of a secular prince. "When I found the Pope's authority highly advanced, and with strong arguments mightily defended," said More, "I said unto his Grace: 'I must put your Highness in remembrance of one thing, and that is this. The Pope, as your Grace knoweth, is a prince as you are, and in league with all other Christian princes. It may hereafter so fall out that your Grace and he may vary upon some points of the league, whereupon may grow breach of amity and war between you both. I think it best, therefore, that the place be amended and his authority more slenderly touched.' "[1]

But Henry refused to make any changes, answering that:

"We are so much bounden to the See of Rome that we
cannot do too much honour unto it." More then reminded
the King of the statute of *Praemunire* by which a good part
of the Pope's pastoral cure here was pared away. To that
answered his Highness: "Whatsoever impediment be to the
contrary, we will set forth that authority to the uttermost,
for we received from that See our Crown imperial."
"Which," added More dryly, "till his Grace with his own
mouth told it me, I never heard of before."[2] The book was
sent to Rome, and there his Ambassador, Master John
Clark, presented it to the Pontiff. The Englishman in a
long speech again emphasized his Sovereign's detestation
of Luther. Leo expressed suitable gratitude and soon
gave form to his thanks by sending to Henry a reward that
was not unexpected. Charles of Spain was called "The
Catholic King"; the King of France bore the title of "Most
Christian." Henry was now informed that "We, the true
successor of St. Peter . . . presiding in this Holy See, from
whence all dignity and titles have their source, having with
our brethren maturely deliberated on these things, and with
one consent unanimously decreed to bestow on your Majesty this title, *viz:* Defender of the Faith. And as we have
by this title honoured you, we likewise command all Christians that they may name your Majesty by this title; and
in their writings to your Majesty that immediately after the
word *KING* they add, *DEFENDER OF THE FAITH* . . ."[3]

There was great glee and celebration at the English
Court, and only the Court Jester was bold enough to de-
ride the Papal honour. "Oh good Henry," said the buffoon,
"let thou and I defend one another, and let the faith alone
to defend itself."

Henry's delight with this new title never faded, and when he broke with Rome he legalized it by an Act of Parliament. Furthermore, it was made hereditary, and to this day Henry's successors have proudly carried the dignity that was bestowed by Pope Leo X.

Luther promptly answered his royal antagonist with a pamphlet filled with vigorous vituperation and vulgar insult. The angry King thought it not wise to lower his dignity by giving a personal reply, so the task was delegated to More, who assumed the pen name of William Ross for the purpose. He wrote in a manner that matched Luther's invective, very unlike his usual style. The words of William Ross were a far cry indeed from the prose of *Four Last Things* which, somehow, More found time to produce around this period. *Four Last Things* was the first of his great essays, contemplative and devotional, a sermon superbly written, illustrating the futility of man's absurd scramble for those things which, with the inevitability of death, he must abandon at the grave.

The vanities and futilities of the Field of the Cloth of Gold provided some of the inspiration for the *Four Last Things*. And so too did the shock of the trial and execution of Edward Stafford, third Duke of Buckingham, which occurred before a year had passed. This nobleman had stood high in the favour of both Henry and his father. He was beloved by the Queen. As Lord Constable of England, he had ridden with Henry on the Field of Gold. He was immensely wealthy and kept a court, complete with a chancellor, of his own. Royal blood was in his veins; a dangerous circumstance when a jealous king, yet without male heir, held the throne. Such a man regarded Wolsey as an upstart and took little pains to conceal a resentment at having to give the precedence and attendance that the Cardinal demanded. On one occasion, at the ceremonial handing of a dish, he had spilled water on the Cardinal's gold slippers and it seemed no accident. He had murmured that Wolsey's extravagance would ruin England, and as a friend of England's Spanish Queen, he had looked with a cold eye on the Cardinal's flirtings with France. He hated the Cardinal with vehemence but with little sense.

A few indiscreet boastings of his royal lineage, a witness who swore that years before he had heard the Duke declare that "if aught but good come to the King, he should be next in blood to the crown" was enough ammunition for his enemy. Jealousy, suspicion, fear, were emotions easy to Henry, and a few words sufficed. The unsuspecting nobleman was sent for and thrown into the Tower. High treason was the charge, the motions of a trial by his peers were made, witnesses were paraded, King and Cardinal waited for the verdict that could not counter their wish. In turn, each of seventeen peers was given the question, and one by one they gave the expected answer. The Duke of Norfolk wept as he told the proud Buckingham that he was to be drawn on a hurdle to the place of execution, there to be hanged, cut down alive, his members to be cut off and cast in the fire, his bowels burnt before his eyes, his head smitten off, his body to be quartered and divided at the King's will.

Buckingham's doom was yet another and important stage in the doctrine of absolutism that Wolsey was teaching the young King. The most powerful nobleman in the kingdom had been struck down without difficulty and under the cloak of legality. As Henry's ferocities and fears increased with his years, this pretence of legal form was a common vehicle for the murders that recurred with pitiless monotony.

The terrible verdict shocked the Queen. Buckingham had been her friend since she had landed in England. His sympathies had been for her interests. And now he was to die! She went to her husband and begged for clemency. Henry, professing to be moved by her tears and supplication, magnanimously said he would show mercy. He commanded that the sentence be voided, save for one thing, the finality of the headsman's axe. Buckingham was taken to Tower Green, and there in the clearness of a late spring morning, he was beheaded.

The execution was unpopular, and in London the mood was sullen. There was much angry talk, and it reached the ears of the King. Ever quick to take alarm, he sent for More and instructed him to convey to the Aldermen a warning of the royal displeasure. Four days later, and still brooding, he again dispatched him to the City. This time More told the Mayor and Aldermen that in order to mollify Henry's anger the harness of the City must be taken to, and exhibited at, certain designated places.

By this time the uncertain peace had ended on the Continent, and the King of France's men had invaded Spain, thereby setting off a twisted chain reaction of hostilities in many places.

Wolsey's diplomatic juggling took him to Calais again. The Cardinal had no need to be instructed as to More's value, but he received a message from the King's secretary which stated: "As old men decay greatly, the King wishes young men to be acquainted with his affairs and desires Wolsey to make Sir William Sandys and Sir Thomas More privy to negotiations at Calais."[4]

Shortly before More sailed, his favourite daughter, Margaret, was married to William Roper. At first it was not entirely clear sailing for the young couple. The cause of disagreement was of great concern to More, for it was discovered that his son-in-law was a militant Protestant, Roper having become infected with Luther's theories in meeting with the German merchants of the Steelyard. He made no attempt to hide his leanings, and in fact was so zealous and loud in his arguments that reports of his heresy were finally made to Wolsey. Because of More, the Cardinal took no action, other than to give the young man a warning. More argued many times with his son-in-law but met with no success, so in a spirit of both exasperation and dejection he went to his daughter. "Meg, I have borne a long time with thy husband," he declared. "I have reasoned and argued with him in those points of religion, and still given him my poor fatherly counsel; but I perceive none of all this able to call him home; and therefore, Meg, I will no longer argue nor dispute with him, but will clean give him over, and get me another while to God and pray for him."[5] Prayer succeeded where eloquence had failed. Roper returned to orthodoxy and once again took his place in the peaceful unity of the house at Chelsea.

In December, 1521, the Pope died, and as the Cardinals gathered to elect his successor, Wolsey's hopes soared high. He had the promises of the French and the Imperial parties, but he was deceived by both, particularly by Charles who, while loudly saying that he favoured Wolsey, was at the same time secretly pushing the interest of his former tutor, the Hollander, Adrian, Cardinal Archbishop of Tortosa.

Actually the Englishman was never given serious consideration at the conclave. The Medici family pressed hard for their candidate; the Emperor brought every interest at his command for his choice. There was deadlock and eleven scrutinies in all before the name of a new pope was announced. It was the Hollander who, in calling himself Adrian VI, was to break a two-hundred-year-old tradition by not changing his name on achieving the tiara. He was an unpopular choice in Rome. The people of the city greeted him coldly, for he was in every way utterly unlike the great prince prelates to whom they were accustomed. Pomp he detested, flattery too, and those noisy and undisciplined crowds of artists and poets and merchants who had fattened on the generosity of former reigns quickly discovered that papal patronage had ceased to be. No lavish court or costly pageants or feasts and games or chances for easy or dubious riches could be expected during the time of this scrupulous northerner who earnestly desired reform and a united and tranquil Christendom. But the obstacles he had inherited proved insurmountable. He was too late, and perhaps it was this realization that hastened his end. He died less than two years after his election.

The conclave that followed the death of this saintly man was soiled with usual intrigue of the times. Once again the Spanish Emperor gave public support to the cause of Wolsey, and once again he betrayed the Englishman. The latter's name, despite his labyrinthine schemes, never received any mention save as a possible candidate in the event of deadlock. After a turbulent fifty days, victory came to the

Medici clan. The cousin of Leo X, Guilio de Medici, was proclaimed Pope Clement VII. He was a cultured man, possessing many personal graces, but in no way equipped to deal with the tremendous and awful responsibilities of his office and time.

Wolsey's failure in Rome, his diplomatic and military entanglements abroad, the antagonism aroused by his constant and importunate demands for more revenue, had not yet curbed him in his own country. But the dark clouds that presaged his downfall were gathering. Lord Henry Algernon Percy, the young son of the fifth Earl of Northumberland, had seen fit to fall in love with one of the Queen's maids-in-waiting. The romance was frowned upon and there was evidence of royal displeasure. Other plans had been made for both the girl and the high-born youth. It has been claimed that the maid had attracted the roving eye of the King. This is improbable, although there might have been some conjecture on his part, for her sister was one of his mistresses. In any event, the lovelorn gallant was hauled before Wolsey. He was soundly berated and sternly ordered to avoid the girl's company. With considerable anguish, the young nobleman accepted the Cardinal's command and abandoned his suit. As for the maid, she was sent to the country, there to languish and suffer the bitterness of humiliation and scorn. Thus was born Anne Boleyn's hatred for Cardinal Wolsey.

Another step in More's advancement came when, because of the Cardinal's influence, he was made Speaker of the House of Commons. More was reluctant to accept the honour and requested that the King should order the Commons to choose another. But both Henry and Wolsey were determined that he should occupy the Chair. His Majesty, by long experience of his service, declared the Cardinal was well acquainted with More's "wit, learning, and discretion, and the Commons had chosen the fittest person of them all to be their Speaker."[6]

Parliament was convened in the Spring of 1523 for the express purpose of replenishing the Exchequer. Wielding his legatine power, Wolsey had already taxed the clergy one half of their revenues spiritual, to be paid in five years. Now he demanded that Parliament should vote a subsidy of eight hundred thousand pounds. There was much complaint and grumbling at this extravagant request. Word of the opposition quickly reached the Cardinal, and thinking to intimidate his opponents he sent word to the Commons that he would appear before them in person. There was some debate in the House then as to "whether it were better but with a few of his Lords (as the most opinion of the House was), or with his whole train royally to receive him?" More was of the latter opinion. "Masters," he declared, "for as much as my Lord Cardinal lately, ye wot well, laid to our charge the lightness of our tongues for things uttered out of this House, it shall not in my mind be amiss with all his pomp to receive him, with his maces, his pillars, his poll-axes, his crosses, his hat, *and* Great Seal too, to the intent, if he find the like fault with us hereafter, we may be the bolder from ourselves to lay the blame on those that his Grace bringeth here with him."[7]

More had his way. The Cardinal was received with pomp. He made his harangue and then, contemptuously breaking procedure, he addressed questions to individual members. A heavy silence greeted his queries. Finally he turned to the Speaker who, in the guise of apology, gently hinted that the Cardinal's presence was no help to his cause. The infuriated Cardinal stalked away, aware that his mild-mannered protégé was refusing to be his creature. Soon after the incident he angrily admonished More: "Would to God you had been at Rome, Master More, when I made you Speaker." "Your Grace not offended," came the urbane reply, "so would I too."[8]

When More had been installed as Speaker, he broke from tradition by boldly making a plea for the freedom of speech in the House. He pointed out that there could be no true debate when minds and tongues were governed by fear. He told the King, "considering that in your high court of parliament is nothing treated but matter of weight and importance concerning your realm and your own royal estate, it could not fail to let and put to silence from the giving of their advice and counsel many of your discreet Commons, to the great hindrance of the common affairs, except that every of your commons were utterly discharged of all doubt and fear, how anything that it should happen them to speak, should happen of your Highness to be taken." To remove all doubt the Speaker pleads that his Majesty "give to all your commons here assembled, your most gracious license and pardon, freely, without doubt of your dreadful displeasure, every man to discharge his conscience, and boldly in everything incident among us to declare his advice; and whatsoever happen any man to say, that it may like your noble Majesty, of your inestimable goodness to take all in good part, interpreting every man's words, how uncunningly soever they be couched, to proceed yet of good zeal towards the profit of your realm and honor of your royal person. . ."⁹

More's brave bid for the privileges of the House of Commons did not incur the wrath of Henry. And apparently Wolsey's anger was of short duration, for soon after the Cardinal recommended that a hundred pounds, then a very considerable sum, should be paid Sir Thomas from the Exchequer as a reward for his parliamentary services.

At one time indeed Wolsey planned to send More as Ambassador to Spain. More's son-in-law was of the opinion that the Cardinal was becoming increasingly dissatisfied with the Speaker's independent conduct and therefore wished him out of the country. In justice to the Cardinal, the mission to the Emperor needed a man of great competence and merit. To More the whole idea was repugnant, and he was bitterly opposed to leaving England and his family again. He appealed to the King, saying that he would do his duty but he was sure that the rigours of a long journey and strange climate would bring him to his grave. Henry, with considerable understanding, was sympathetic to the plea. "It is not our meaning, Master More, to do you hurt, but to do you good would we be glad; we will therefore for this purpose devise upon some other, and employ your service otherwise."¹⁰

A Humanist friend of More, the kindly Cuthbert Tunstall, was elected to take his place, and soon he was giving evidence that More had not been wrong concerning the dangers of the journey. One of the English envoys, Sir Richard Winfield, Chancellor of the Duchy of Lancaster, died because of sudden sickness contracted in the unaccustomed heat. The following day, Tunstall reported, Mr. Sampson "fell into a fever and is not yet well recovered. I was, not long before Mr. Winfield's sickness, brought so low by a flux that my legs began to fail me. And my stomach and strength was gone. If the fever had come . . . surely I had not escaped."[11]

These were bright and prosperous days for More. Preferment brought gifts of money and grants of land. Already High Steward of the University of Oxford, he was also given the same appointment at Cambridge. He was Collector of Subsidy in Middlesex, and in 1525 he succeeded the unfortunate Winfield as Chancellor of the Duchy of Lancaster. It was he, a few years earlier, who had been chosen to make the speech of welcome when the Emperor Charles had come to London. The warmth of the royal favour even extended to his aged father. Judge More was made one of the "Triers of Petitions for Gascony," an office of considerable dignity. The pressure of his many duties forced More eventually to resign the Under-Treasurership, for he was one of the Council which was required to be in a daily attendance upon the King.

These also were happy days for More's own little realm. Shortly following his return from Cambrai More had moved his family from Bucklersbury to Chelsea. His new house was surrounded by a large garden and farm and was fully equipped to meet the needs of his growing children. It was a beautiful place bordering the Thames, close enough to the City, yet with the greenness and seclusion of the country. Here he was the firm ruler, the loving parent, the scholar, the philosopher, the best of hosts to a constant stream of guests. Even the King, on a sudden whim, would come over to this house at Chelsea, and be merry, dining without previous invitation or notice. On one of these occasions the enthralled family was delighted to see the King stroll with More in the garden for an hour or so, engrossed in happy talk, the royal arm thrown around the commoner's shoulder. When Henry departed, the impressed Roper complimented his father-in-law saying, "how happy he was whom the King had so familiarly entertained, as I never had seen him to do to any except Cardinal Wolsey, whom I saw once walk with arm in arm."

In his reply, More showed well his evaluation of the friendship of princes and, in particular, his own Prince. "I thank our Lord, son," he said, "I find his Grace my very good Lord indeed; and, I believe he doth as singularly favour me as any subject within this realm. Howbeit, son Roper, I may tell thee I have no cause to be proud thereof; for if my head [could] win him a castle in France . . . it should not fail to go."[12]

Once again he was stressing his opinions as to the uncertain permanence of material success. As a young man he had written in his *Book of Fortune:*

"Build not thine house on height up to the sky.
None falleth far, but he that climbeth high.
Remember, Nature sent thee hither bare;
The gifts of Fortune—count them borrowed ware."

The happy days at Chelsea were immortalized by the gifted hand of Hans Holbein. He came as a guest, and his stay resulted in the famous painting of More, the equally famous Family Group, and individual portraits of other members of the family. Erasmus had recommended Holbein to their mutual friend, Peter Giles, as "the man who painted me; I will not trouble you with a testimonial, but he is a great man at his craft. . ." Upon Holbein's arrival, More agreed with his friend: "Your painter, dearest Erasmus, is a wonderful man; but I fear he won't find England as fruitful as he had hoped. Yet I will do my best to see that he does not find it absolutely barren."[13]

At the end of his two years' leave Holbein returned to Basel and purchased for himself a house with his English money. But it was posterity which profited most by his stay in the More household.

10

SIR THOMAS MORE was in his forty-seventh year when in 1525 he was given the Chancellorship of the Duchy of Lancaster. Wolsey was fifty-two. Henry was thirty-four. His Queen was six years older. Her maid-in-waiting, Anne Boleyn, was eighteen. And Anne's elder sister was still, occasionally, the King's mistress.

The Cardinal was still bleeding the Treasury to keep English troops on French soil. In the long dreary war between France and Spain, victory had come suddenly to the Emperor Charles. The French King was captured at Pavia. There was rejoicing at the English court but not in Wolsey's heart. England's ally, nephew of Catherine, betrothed to the child Princess Mary, the Prince who had deceived Wolsey, and therefore England, at two conclaves, was now too strong, too independent. Fresh moves were needed in the Cardinal's shifty political game. He looked across the Channel, mind working, plans brewing.

The Emperor brought no ease to the mounting tension. The tie that bound Spain to England was his betrothal pact with the daughter of Henry and Catherine. But the little Princess Mary was only nine years old and Charles had another bride in mind. Isabella of Portugal was beautiful, nearer his own age, and possessed of a dowry of nine hundred thousand golden ducats in ready cash. He sent an Ambassador to England with a request that his betrothal be broken or that the child Princess be sent to Spain at once and with a huge cash dowry. Henry listened to the Spanish envoy in a cold fury. He deemed the proposal to be a personal and national insult. The betrothal was broken. The Emperor was free to marry the Portuguese Princess. The link between Spain and England was snapped. Wolsey was now encouraged to deal with France. And while England's Spanish-born Queen brooded and lamented over the change, her husband, as though both to humiliate her and emphasize his hatred of Spanish influence, brought to Court the bastard son whom he had sired by Elizabeth Blount. The little boy, who was called Henry Fitzroy, was now six years old. He was living proof to his father that he could produce a male heir. It was a Queen's duty, no less than a King's, to provide a son for the succession. And in this she had failed. Ten years of tragic miscarriages had given the dynasty but one surviving child, a daughter—and she half-Spanish at that. England was not yet reconciled to the idea of a ruling Queen. There must be a Prince to take up the scepter, and Catherine was now past the child-bearing stage.

CLEMENT VII

Henry looked at his small son thoughtfully. He knighted him, and as soon as the dubbing was completed the lad was put before two earls and made a peer of the realm with the title of Earl of Nottingham. This was not all. The new Earl was then created Duke of Richmond and Somerset and to complement this rank, further dignities were to be conferred. He was to be Lord Admiral of England, Wales, and Ireland, of Normandy, Gascony and Aquitaine. He was to be a Knight of the Garter, Keeper of the City and Castle of Carlisle, and he was to take precedence as first peer of England. There was only one title lacking, that of Wales, already borne by the nine-year-old Mary, and it would seem that Henry wished Elizabeth Blount's son to be next King.

And there were other thoughts simmering in the royal mind. That peculiar apparatus, his conscience, was astir. Was not his marriage to Catherine, his brother's widow, a violation of the Levitical law? It was true that the Pope had given a dispensation permitting the marriage. Testimony had been sworn that Catherine's union with Arthur had never been consummated. But were all the facts truly known? Now that his friendship with the Spanish Emperor was terminated, it was possible, and very convenient, to think that a terrible mistake might have been made, a grievous sin committed. Henry muttered his scruples to his confessor and reminded him that the respected Archbishop Warham had voiced concern at the time of the marriage.

The alert ears of Wolsey caught the whisper. It has been charged, but not proved, that it was he who planted the thought. Henry's "scruple" may have been born as early as 1522. A few years later, after the Emperor's victory, the whole idea could certainly be regarded by the Cardinal with considerable favour. Friendship with France was his course. The French King's sister was unmarried. If it were made possible for Henry to take her as a bride, strong cement indeed would be poured into the foundations of the new alliance. And if a male heir came from such a marriage, Henry would be happy and the Tudor dynasty would be assured. It was an inviting mirage, with unlimited possibilities.

In her chapel, Catherine, now separated from her daughter by Henry's orders, spent long hours in prayer, as well she might, for the King's "Secret Matter" was fast losing its secrecy and quickly becoming his "Great Matter."

Sir Thomas, strolling by the banks of the river with his son-in-law, suddenly remarked: "Now would to Our Lord . . . upon condition that three things were well established in Christendom, I were put in a sack and here presently cast into the Thames."

"What great things be those, Sir?" asked the young man, "that should move you so to wish?"

"In faith, son, they be these," replied More.

"The first is that whereas the most part of Christian princes be at mortal war, they were all at an universal peace. The second, that where the Church of Christ is, at this present, sore afflicted with many errors and heresies, it were well settled in a perfect uniformity of religion. The third, that where the king's matter of his marriage is now come in question, it were to the glory of God and quietness of all parties brought to a good conclusion."[1]

The seed of the great schism had been sown by 1526, yet in that year nobody foresaw the rapidity with which

Henry would move to deny allegiance to Rome. But the Cardinal set before his Master, never a dull pupil, a daily and dangerous example: as Legate and Lord Chancellor, he demonstrated that authority over Church and State could be vested in one person. He furnished continuous proof to a greedy sovereign that heavy taxes could be levied on the clergy and that ready monies could be gained by suppressing monasteries. He was also, by his almost incredible pomps and vanities, his ruthless rule and conduct, fomenting a general hatred not only towards the entire clerical state but towards the Pope he professed to represent.

No tinge of Lutheranism was in Henry's new bent. He was, as he always so fervently protested, the pious, the militant Catholic, making his confessions, attending his daily Mass, damning the heresy that was erupting and spreading from Germany. He applauded and gave vast encouragement to More, whose pen was enlisted for the defence of Catholicity, even while the passions and forces that were to tear England from the Church mounted. "You cannot spend the occasional hours which you can steal from your official duties better," Tunstall wrote to More in 1527, "than in composing in your own language such books as may show to simple and unlearned men the cunning malice of the heretics and fortify them against the impious subverters of the Church."[2]

More listened to the arguments that had sprung from across the sea and made his first rebuttal in *The Dialogue Against Heresies,* sometimes referred to as *Quoth He and Quoth I.* It was a lengthy work, divided into four books. With wit, scholarship and ability he defended the Catholic position, answering point by point all charges. He admitted

the necessity for reform in the Church and the weaknesses
of the clergy, but he maintained that there were good and
there were bad in all professions. If clergymen were familiar, they were called light; if they were solitary, they were
regarded as fantastic; if they were sad, they were called
solemn; if they were merry, they were regarded as mad;
if they were holy, they were called hypocrites; if they kept
few servants, they were called niggards; if they kept many,
they were pompous. He had not said that they were all
faultless nor had he excused their faults. But if the bishops,
he said, would take into the priesthood better and fewer
laymen, all the matter would be more than half amended.

His calm reasoning was always marked by his humour.
To Luther's assertion that it was not necessary to confess
to a priest, that a friend, either man or woman, would suffice, More made the gay reply that if a pretty woman could
hear confessions then many a man who formerly had delayed the duty would find it easy frequently to ease his
conscience. To the Lutheran theory of predestination he
told the story of a thief who at his trial defended himself
on the grounds that he had been predestined to steal. But
the judge replied that predestination also governed his actions. He had been predestined to sentence the thief to the
gallows. For those who attacked the validity of miracles,
More told a sweet story and gravely gave assurance of his
personal knowledge and authentication of the miracle and
those persons connected with it. In the village of St. Stephen's a young couple were married, and soon after "the
seed of them twain turned in the woman's body into blood
and after into shape of man child." In less than a year a
boy child was born, "and forsooth it was not then passing

the length of a foot." But a miracle has occurred, for the infant is now taller than More himself. When it is asked how long ago this incident took place, the solemn answer is "By my faith, about twenty-one years."

This phase of More's championship of the Church was to last about six years. He was a layman, but he became the principal defender of the Spirituality. "The bishop's proctor," as he was called by his antagonists, was drawn into the controversy only because of a high sense of duty, for it was he who wrote:

> *When a hatter*
> *Will go smatter*
>   *In philosophy,*
> *Or a pedlar*
> *Wax a meddler*
>   *In theology*
> *All that ensue*
> *Such crafts new*
>   *They drive so far a cast*
> *That ever more*
> *They do therefore*
>   *Beshrew themselves at last.*[3]

In the long literary controversy, four men led the lists against More: William Tyndale, John Frith, Simon Fish, and Christopher Saint-German. The first two were priests, influenced by the new heresy; the second two were lawyers. All four were able men and put their cases well, but their opponent was abler still. After completing the *Dialogue,* More answered Fish's *Supplication of Beggars* with *Sup-*

plication of Souls. Again he showed his characteristic wit in the story of "a lewd gallant and a good friar. Whom, when the gallant saw going barefoot in a great frost and snow, he asked him why he did take such pain. And he answered that it was very little pain if a man would remember hell. 'Yea, Friar,' quod the gallant, 'but what and there be no hell? Then art thou a great fool?' 'Yea, Master,' quod the friar, 'but what and there be hell? Then is your mastership a much more fool'."[4]

Even when he became Lord Chancellor, More somehow found time to wield his pen in defence of the Church, nor after his fall from the high office was the labour diminished. The pen continued to move; book after book answered the arguments and charges of the enemy. He deemed the great task he had undertaken to be both a duty and a work of love, and to keep his moral independence he avoided subsidy.

After her romance with the young Percy had been broken and she had been sent to languish in the country, very little is known of Anne Boleyn's activities or whereabouts for a few years. Equal mystery surrounds the date of her return to Court. Bishop Burnet, in his *History of the Reformation*, claims that she was sent to France after the end of the War and did not return to England until 1527. This is doubtful. Another source states that in order to avoid the King's attentions her father kept her secluded in the country. This also is doubtful. Sir Thomas Boleyn was no man to cross his prince. He had with the highest degree of equanimity seen his eldest daughter debauched by Henry. There was no reason why he should object to Anne accepting the same role. He was ambitious and unscrupulous,

and during the little-known period of Anne's life he sought
and received favour from Henry. He was made Treasurer
of the Household, an appointment which carried rich revenues. He became Steward and Chamberlain at Tunbridge,
receiver and bailiff of Bradsted, keeper of the manor of
Penshurst, keeper of the parks of Thundersly, Essex and
Westwood. He was one of Henry's boisterous drinking and
hunting companions, and sometimes he served him as an
Ambassador. In 1525 he was raised to the peerage with the
title of Viscount Rochford.

It can be assumed that Anne was once again a maid-in-
waiting to Catherine some time after 1525 and that as such
she would be seen almost daily by Henry. This was the
time when his "conscience" was troubling him concerning
the validity of his marriage, and this was the time when he
set in motion the machinery that was to satisfy his scruples
and, eventually, his passion for Anne.

The capture and snaring of the King by Anne was not
sudden. It was a slow and deliberate process. She had no
wish to suffer her sister's fate, to be merely one of the royal
mistresses, subject to whim and caprice, cast off and married to a complacent subject when Henry had tired of her.
She was determined that this would not be her fate, and
with an amazing blend of will power and shrewdness she
succeeded. For six years she held off the eager monarch,
tantalizing him, inviting him, promising him, but never
surrendering until her audacious goal was in sight. Her
game was probably one of the most skillful and prolonged
feats of coquetry ever to be perpetrated. One ponders over
the secret of her success, the taming and subjugation of this
lustful and willful creature who never before had been

tamed or thwarted in any of his desires, let alone in the lists of love. What magic did she wield to make the Defender of the Faith break with Rome, reject his Queen, bring ruin and disgrace to Wolsey, his lifelong friend and chief adviser?

She was pretty, but not extraordinarily so, if we may judge by her portraits and the testimony of acquaintances, both hostile and friendly. But the written word, the brush and paint often fail to convey the dimension and measure of that peculiar and fatal attraction with which a woman can enthrall a man. She was slim in body and possessed of masses of thick, dark, lustrous hair. Her eyes were almond-shaped, sparkling black in colour, ready to dance with mischief, and equally ready to mirror her opposite moods. One hand was blemished by an additional nail, but by dexterity and cleverness she concealed this defect. She certainly was not beautiful in the conventional sense of the word, but beauty in the realm of amour is the property and endowment of the participants alone. Under the spell of emotion they dwell and move in an enchanted world of their own, confusing realities with dreams, peering at each other through the dangerous and distorted lens of guile and passion. It has ever been and ever will be.

At the Mardi Gras festivities in 1526, Henry flaunted a motto "Declare I dare not." Perhaps this was a message to the girl who still attended his wife. As for Anne, she certainly returned the look. She, of a certainty, plied all the devices of flirtation and coquetry, but steadfastly she held away from him. The enamoured monarch floundered deeper and deeper in the mire of his infatuation, becoming increasingly desperate, increasingly firm in his resolve to possess and own her. She still held away, but as though to show him the road she sent him a brooch that was a symbol in jewels of her position and ambition. The bauble represented a lone maid in a ship, and it carried the significant motto: "There or nowhere."

When the spring warmth of the year 1527 came to dispel the wet chill from London roofs and streets, the King's "Great Matter" was the exciting and public gossip of the crowded city. Everywhere, in the taverns, in the merchants' courtyards, in the artisans' shops, on the wharves, the subject was discussed and surmise made. Henry alone thought the business to be a secret. In April he was telling the French Ambassador, "I have certain things to communicate to your master, of which Wolsey knows nothing."

It is hard to believe that the astute Cardinal was unaware of something which was an open secret to everybody else. The important point of Henry's statement, terribly important to the Cardinal—and, indeed, to history—was the fact that the King, for a first time, was acting independently of the Cardinal and dealing directly with a foreign prince.

The goad of his frustrated passion spurred the hot-blooded King to action. On May 8, Wolsey was summoned to the royal presence and officially told of the King's doubts concerning the validity of his marriage and therefore the uncertain status of the succession. Nothing was said of Anne Boleyn, and in this the Cardinal was fooled. Even if he knew, as he probably did, of Henry's infatuation, he put it down as being a matter of no importance, a passing interlude among many such incidents in the crowded career of a practising sensualist. The Cardinal pondered over the King's words on that May afternoon and then made his decision, and his mistake. There would be difficulties in dissolving the marriage. That he perceived, but he also knew the fierce and unbridled will of the King. He would obey his master and, at the same time, channel events to serve England's interests in France. Catherine was of little political importance since her nephew, the Spanish Emperor, had severed his link with England. Alliance with France was a thing to be desired. The nimble brain of the Cardinal worked swiftly as he bowed low before his sovereign. He acted with speed.

Within a fortnight, Wolsey, acting as Legate, convened a Court of Justice to determine the status of Henry's marriage. The Archbishop of Canterbury, Warham, acted as assessor. The King was solemnly charged "to answer for eighteen years' sinful cohabitation with Catherine." The object of the "trial" was to find error with and pronounce invalid that dispensation of Pope Julius II which had enabled Henry to marry his brother's widow. The usual legality was thrown over the proceedings. An attorney was appointed to "defend" the King. A Dr. Wolman was made promoter or prosecutor. The whole affair was supposed to be kept a secret, but it was of a size too big to be confined to a corner.

All London rocked with the gossip. Sympathy was with the Queen. Tankards were raised to her health and honour. Wolsey was blamed. Ever unpopular, he was jeered and mocked when his stately processions disturbed the traffic of the narrow streets. When the news reached Catherine, she acted with courage and promptness. Off sped a message to Spain. She had been born a Princess of Aragon. She had been a good wife and a good Queen. Now to be told that she was neither, that her daughter was illegitimate, was unthinkable. The Pope must be informed. Wolsey must be curbed.

The conspiracy failed. The court did not, as had been the intention, heartily proclaim Henry to be a bachelor. There was much talk and delay, and, fume though Henry might, the slow forms of a trial followed. Episcopal opinion was invited. The bishops were mostly products of lay investiture. As such they wore their mitres because of the King's favour, but the pull of duty was still towards Rome. The powerful prelate, John Fisher, Bishop of Rochester and close friend of More's, was outspoken in his belief that the marriage was indissoluble. Torn between conflicting loyalties, the bewildered and worried tribunal decided that before a definite decision could be made, the sham secrecy would have to be abandoned, and that both the Pope and Catherine be notified.

While these proceedings were yet under way there came, with the dramatic suddenness of a thunderclap, startling news from Italy, news that was to make useless any continuance of the so-called trial. Mercenary troops of the Emperor, unafraid and without discipline, without strategy or direction, had marched upon Rome and given sack to the city. The unbridled mob, for mob this army became, breached the walls, and in a frenzy wreaked violence and brutality of every description upon the ancient scene. The rich treasures of the Renaissance were a wild invitation for looting. Terrified citizenry were murdered in crowds with a particular ferocity, their wives and daughters raped even as their houses were fired and gutted. Religion was no shield in this mad debauch of blood. Cardinals were flogged and dragged along the streets, priests were slaughtered before their altars, nuns were violated in the cloister. The Pope sought hurried refuge behind the thick walls of the Castle of St. Angelo and there, his ears still echoing with cries of the dying and the yells of assassins, he realized that he was cut off from Christendom, a prisoner of the Emperor. And it was from this unfortunate and helpless pontiff that Henry was seeking permission to divorce and humiliate the Emperor's aunt.

The new state of affairs was quickly and well understood in England, but it brought no change to Henry's wishes. The Pope might be surrounded by a marauding horde, but the King of England was the prisoner of a more dangerous captor; he was a slave to the bent and sway of his own passion. Wolsey was berated, the trial was discreetly dissolved to a nothing, and while the Cardinal, ever his master's servant, pondered over new plans, Henry tried a different tactic. He went to his Queen, and, on his knees, begged her understanding and sympathy. Catherine was a religious woman, and it was religion that he used as the theme of his supplication. He quoted the passage from the Book of Leviticus. He told of the learned clerics whom he had consulted. He swore that it was nothing but scruple and conscience which was driving him to ask her to accept separation and leave the Court. He prated of mortal sin and recited a long history of sleepless nights. The whole troublesome matter could be solved, he gently hinted, if she discreetly retired and entered a convent. But retreat from trouble, talk of scruple and conscience were arguments that only served to strengthen Catherine's belief in her own position. She also had scruple and conscience. She had been a good and loyal wife. She knew her marriage was valid and she declared it would be an irremediable wrong if she said otherwise. She would not bastardize her daughter. Her vows had been solemnly made before God and, for better or for worse, her place was by her husband's side. Defeated and for once abashed, Henry backed his bulk from her presence, muttering a request that for the moment she say nothing of his plea.

11

MEANWHILE, Wolsey's new strategy was taking form. The Sack of Rome had begun on the ninth of May. By July the third, the Cardinal had made his arrangements and was able to depart from London for France, where he hoped to ratify a new treaty, ironical in name, of perpetual peace. It was to be his last journey abroad, but he travelled with his usual pomp and glitter. An army of servants, richly dressed in black velvet, left Westminster with him. A troop of nine hundred horse gave escort to his crimson- and gilt-caparisoned mule. His silver crosses and pillars, the Great Seal of England, the Cardinal's Hat, were carried in their accustomed places. There was a long train of carts and carriages. There were spearmen and archers. There were the haughty gentlemen of his household, and riding close by the scarlet magnificence was soberly-dressed Thomas More, quietly observing everything, disliking the idea of leaving England but obeying a command to employ his skill at the forthcoming negotiations. Closely guarded by men-at-arms was a paymaster and barrels of gold, for Wolsey was determined to leave little to chance in his bid for friendship with the French.

The second night from London he stopped at Rochester, where he was a guest of John Fisher in the Bishop's palace. Fisher was the firmest supporter of the Queen's position in the English hierarchy, and the Cardinal sought to change his opinion. More was a friend of Fisher's, but he was not invited to the conferences between the two prelates. They talked in secret until late at night, but Fisher remained of the same mind. In the morning the Cardinal set out again for the sea. At Canterbury the stately train paused, and there were services held for the Pope. Wolsey gave orders that the choir should sing *Ora pro papa nostro Clemente* instead of the usual *Ora pro nobis*. He wept as he prayed, and well might he shed tears. The plight of his spiritual master was sorry enough, and surely by this time his astute mind had some foreboding of the fatal road along which his temporal master was forcing him.

A large fleet took the glittering and unwieldy embassy across the Channel. At Amiens he met Francis with full pomp and ceremony. The procession that entered the French city was two miles long. He insisted that the French King dismount and accord him ·the greeting of a fellow monarch. Pageantry was met with pageantry. He dispensed indulgences with a lavish hand, and he was given the privilege of freeing prisoners. The Cathedral bells tolled a thunderous salute to the last of his great excursions. The discussions concerning the proposed Treaty began, and the Cardinal introduced a plan which was staggering in its audacity and scope. He proposed that, because the Pope was a prisoner of the Emperor, a Council of the Church should be convened at Avignon. There, those high prelates who were not under Spanish domination would meet with him, Wolsey, presiding and acting in effect as vice-regent for the enslaved pontiff. Wielding the papal power, he could accomplish many things, not least among them the granting of divorce. Henry then would be free to marry Francis' sister, the French and English thrones would be bound in permanent alliance, and thus the Treaty between the two countries firmly cemented. The fantastic scheme did not meet with success, and despite every device of statecraft that he could muster, the French King and his Cardinals, while courting and accepting the Treaty, evaded the proposed usurpation of papal authority.

Even at this date the Cardinal was unaware of the extent of Henry's passion. He who thought he knew every move of his master certainly must have known of the King's infatuation, but he continued to assume that Anne, like her sister, was merely another royal mistress. That her intentions were directed beyond the bed and at the throne was something which did not enter his imagination. But while he treated with the French, Henry plunged deeper into his folly. The skill of Anne's coquetry was amazing. She could tantalize the lusty, headstrong King into giving wild protestations of his feelings for her, yet she was able to hold him off without inviting that quick rage which was so common to him. When he was not by her side his inflamed emotions forced him to concoct extravagant protestations of his aching devotion for her. "I beseech you now," he wrote, "with the greatest earnestness to let me know your whole intention as to the love between us two. For I must of necessity obtain this answer of you; having been for above a whole year struck with the dart of love, and not yet sure whether I shall fail, or find a place in your heart and affection . . . I beg you to give an entire answer to this my rude letter, that I may know on what and how far I may depend; but if it does not please you to answer me in writing, let me know some place where I may have it by word of mouth, and I will go thither with all my heart . . . Written by the hand of him who would willingly remain yours, —H. Rex."[1]

Five more impassioned letters went to Anne during the same hot summer month. The second began with the traditional complaint of the anxious lover: "Although, my mistress, you have not been pleased to remember the promise which you made me when I was last with you, which was that I should hear news of you, and have an answer to my last letter, yet I think it belongs to a true servant (since otherwise he can know nothing) to send to enquire of a mistress' health; and, for to acquit myself of the office of a true servant, I send you this letter, begging you to give me an account of the state you are in, which I pray God may continue as long in prosperity, as I wish my own; and that you may the oftener remember me, I send you by this bearer a buck killed late last night by my hand, hoping when you eat of it you will think on the hunter; and thus for want of more room I will make an end of my letter. Written by the hand of your servant, who often wishes you in your brother's room."[2]

The Boleyns, father, brother, uncle, together with their

sympathizers were now a most powerful influence at Court. They hated the Cardinal, but they still feared him. With intense interest they watched the King's wooing. A few days after he had sent Anne the trophy of his hunting prowess, his pen was again busy in a fervent plea: "I and my heart put ourselves in your hands, begging you to recommend us to your favour, and not to let absence lessen your affection to us. For it were great pity to increase our pain, which absence alone does sufficiently, and more than I could ever have thought; bringing to my mind a point of astronomy, which is, That the longer the Moors are from us, the farther too is the sun, and yet his heat is the more scorching; so it is with our love; we are at a distance from one another, and yet it keeps its fervency, at least on my side. I hope the like on your part, assuring you that the uneasiness of absence is already too severe for me; and when I think of the continuance of that which I must of necessity suffer, it would seem intolerable to me, were it not for the firm hope I have of your unchangeable affection for me; and now to put you sometimes in mind of it, seeing I cannot be present in person with you, I send you the nearest thing to that possible, that is, my picture set in bracelets . . . " [3]

Another letter, written before the month had closed, is not as happy. In it can be detected some hint of the provocative game that Anne is playing. She had apparently exercised the feminine prerogative, for Henry was fretful "because, since my last parting with you I have been told that you have entirely changed the opinion in which I left you, and that you would neither come to Court with your mother, nor any other way; which report, if true, I cannot enough wonder at, being persuaded in my own mind that I have never committed any offence against you; and it seems a very small return for the great love I bear you, to be kept at a distance from the person and presence of a woman in the world that I value the most; and if you love me with as much affection as I hope you do, I am sure, the distance of our two persons would be a little uneasy to you: though this does not belong so much to the mistress as the servant. Consider well, my mistress, how greatly your absence grieves me . . ."[4]

The days pass and the pendulum of his passion swings him to a more pleasant mood. In fervent declaration Anne is told that "the demonstrations of your affection are such, the fine thoughts of your letter so cordially expressed, that they oblige me forever to honour, love and serve you sincerely, beseeching you to continue in the same firm and constant purpose, and assuring you, that, on my part, I will not only make you a suitable return, but outdo you in loyalty of heart, if it be possible. I desire you also, that if at any time before this I have in any sort offended you, you would give me the same absolution which you ask, assuring you that hereafter my heart shall be dedicated to you alone; I wish my body was so too; God can do it, if he pleases, to whom I pray once a day for that end; hoping that at length my prayers will be heard. I wish the time may be short, but I shall think it long, till we shall see one another. Written by the hand of the secretary, who in heart, body and will is your loyal and most assured servant . . ."[5]

More's embassy occupied the whole summer and culminated in a Solemn Mass at the Cathedral of Amiens on August 17, 1527. Upon More's return to England he was summoned to appear before the King at Hampton Court.

The impatient lover undoubtedly thought that the fore-most lawyer of the land would assist in the strategy of his "Great Matter." He made no mention of Anne Boleyn. Conscience and scruple were his song. He flourished a Bible and quoted the familiar passage from Leviticus. He claimed precedent for authority and recited a list of pre-vious annulments. He related the circumstances of his mar-riage, of how, before the wedding ceremony, he had made objection. He reminded More that Archbishop Warham had, at the same time, also expressed uneasiness. The King was eloquent and he had grounds for argument. But More pleaded that he was "unmeet to meddle in such matters" and that it was a question to be solved by the proper canonists and theologians. Such a reply did not suit Henry, for he wanted the weight of More's opinion on his side. He ordered More to consult with the Bishops of Durham and Bath. More obeyed, but again insisted on his ineligibility. He referred to the teachings of St. Augustine and St. Jerome and other great Doctors of the Church. He explained to Henry that "to be plain with your Grace, neither my Lord of Durham nor my Lord of Bath, though I know them both to be wise, virtuous, learned and honourable prelates, nor myself, with the rest of your Council, being all your Grace's own servants, for your manifold benefits daily bestowed on us so most bounden to you, be, in my judgment, meet counsellors for your Grace herein."[6]

It was an unsatisfactory answer and a highly dangerous way to treat with Henry. When thwarted, he fell into a rage, but such was More's conciliatory and reasonable attitude, and so highly did the King regard him, that he showed no resentment either at this time or on certain future occasions when he could choose to discuss the subject again. Always, as was his duty, More listened to his monarch's arguments, but never once did he change his opinions nor declare for the divorce.

Wolsey's tactics were proving too slow and tedious for Henry. While the Cardinal was still parleying in France, Henry decided to send his secretary, Dr. Knight, to Rome, and there procure from the beleaguered Pope a special dispensation which would allow him to marry again without a formal annulment of his marriage with Catherine. This hasty and bigamous proposal was doomed from the beginning, but it was the act which marked Henry's first deliberate step away from Wolsey.

Dr. Knight's mission was supposed to be secret, but the Cardinal, with his agents everywhere, quickly was aware of what was happening. He met Knight in France, and after much questioning learned the whole story. For the first time probably he realized the scope of Henry's infatuation. If he entertained any lingering doubts concerning Anne's status, they were certainly dispelled when he came back to England.

The King was in residence at Richmond, and there the Cardinal hurried to make his report. It was the last day of September, and on his arrival, following the usual custom, he requested a private audience. It was not Henry but Anne who gave the loud answer: "Where else is the Cardinal to come? Tell him that he may come here where the King is."[7] And so he was received, not in private, but in the great hall, the young girl defiantly standing by the King's side, a crowd of courtiers smirking and staring at the discomfiture of the haughty and hated prelate. Before this audience, the shocked

Cardinal bent to the royal presence and gave account of his embassy. It was a triumphant moment for Anne, the humiliation of the great man who had so despotically broken her romance with young Lord Percy. In the heady intoxication of her sway over the King, she acted in a manner that the royal-born Catherine, his Queen, had never attempted.

The episode at Richmond invited endless conjecture. Sir Thomas More could not but know of the whole sorry business. He kept aloof from the chatter of the Court. He was in the service of the King, but he was no courtier. He had his many official duties to perform, and his pen, whenever he could seize an hour, was busily employed in arguments against Tyndale and the others of heretical bent. He had explained his position to the King concerning the divorce, and as yet there was no resentment in that quarter. Queen Catherine said that the King had "but one sound councillor in his kingdom, Sir Thomas More." He steadfastly clung to his opinion that an annulment of marriage was a problem to be solved by proper ecclesiastical authority. Neither Wolsey nor the Boleyn faction had any great affection for More, but both recognized his ability, his fame for honesty and scholarship. Wolsey had brought him into the King's service, but he had proved to be no lackey, and on several occasions there had been clashes between the two. About this time there were discussions concerning the draft of a treaty. There were differences of opinion, and the Cardinal had angrily shouted at More: "You show yourself to be a stupid and foolish Councillor." For answer Sir Thomas, who seldom lost his temper, had merely smiled and replied:

"Thanks be to God, that the King's Majesty has but one fool in his Council."[8]

While Wolsey busied himself with the murky drag of a divorce, More was forced to leave England again. The King sent him to Cambrai along with his friend Tunstall, Bishop of Durham. Here the chimera of peace was pursued with a diligence that brought to England the longest freedom from foreign wars in the reign of Henry VIII. For thirteen years, English soldiery did not fire cannon, wield sword, or bend bow on European soil.

More's accomplishment at Cambrai added to his fame at home. Roper records that he "so worthily handled himself, procuring in our league far more benefits unto this realm than at that time by the King or his Council was thought possible to be compassed, that for his good service in that voyage, the King, when he after made him Lord Chancellor, caused the Duke of Norfolk openly to declare unto the people (as you shall hear hereafter) (more at large) how much all England was bound unto him."[9]

More composed his own epitaph, and he thought enough of his work at Cambrai to mention it alone of his diplomatic service. He wrote that "he both joyfully saw and was present ambassador when the leagues between the chief princes of Christendom were renewed again, and peace, so long looked for, restored to Christendom. Which peace our Lord stable and make perpetual."[10]

When negotiations at Cambrai had been concluded, More went back to England and made his report to the King, who was at Woodstock. While this was happening he received news of a calamity which had befallen his beloved home at Chelsea. There had been a fire and much damage. The letter he sent to his wife is a magnificent mirroring of his philosophy, his piety, his kindness. "I am informed by my son Heron of the loss of our barns," he wrote, "and our neighbours' also, with all the corn that was therein, albeit (saving God's pleasure) it is great pity of so much good corn lost, yet since it hath liked him to send us such a chance, we must not only be content, but also be glad of his visitation. He sent us all that we have lost: and since he hath by such a chance taken it away again, his pleasure be fulfilled. Let us not grudge thereat, but take it in good worth, and heartily thank him, as well for adversity, as for prosperity. And for adventure we have more cause to thank him for our loss, than for our winning. For his wisdom better seeth what is good for us than we do ourselves. Therefore I pray you be of good cheer, and take all the household with you to church, and there thank God both for that he hath given us, and for that he hath left us, which if it please him, he can increase when he will. And if it please him to leave us yet less, at his pleasure be it. I pray you to make some good search with what my poor neighbours have lost, and bid them take no thought therefore, and if I should not leave myself a spoon, there shall no poor neighbour of mine bear no loss by chance happened in my house. I pray you be with my children and household merry in God. And devise some-what with your friends, what way were best to take, for provision to be made for corn for our household, and for seed this year coming, if ye think it good that we keep the ground still in our hands. And whether ye think it good why we shall do or not, yet I think it were not best suddenly thus to leave it all up, and to put away our folk of our farm, till we have somewhat advised us thereon . . . I would not any man were suddenly sent away he knows not whither." He had tarried with the King's grace. But now, because of this chance, he thought to get leave "this next week to come home and see you; and then shall we further devise together upon all things, what order shall be best to take; and thus as heartily fare you well with all our children as you can wish . . ."[11]

After More had reported on his negotiations abroad he was given permission to join his family, while Henry, with Anne ever by his side and her coterie in favour, moved the Court back to Richmond, and then to Greenwich; all the time feverishly pressing for the dissolution of his marriage.

Pope Clement VII was greatly distressed. England's schism was now perceptible, but evident too was the watchful interest and ever-ready displeasure of Catherine's nephew, the Emperor. Clement was a weak man, and, caught between the two forces, he sought a solution in procrastination. He deferred answer to Henry, thinking perhaps, that the royal passion might ebb with the passing of time.

Knight's mission to Italy having proved valueless, Wolsey dispatched abler men, Stephen Gardiner and Edward Fox. They arrived at Orvieto and were received by Clement on March 20th, 1528. The Pope's quarters in this mean town were vastly different from the magnificences of the Vatican. "The Court here is bankrupt," reported an envoy; "the bishops go about on foot in tattered cloaks; the courtiers take flight in despair."[12] Cried the unhappy Pontiff: "They have plundered me of all I possess, even the canopy above my bed is not mine, it is borrowed."[13] Short of food, short of drinking water even, shorn of all vestige of temporal power, confined to his bed because of crippled feet, this perplexed successor of St. Peter greeted the English agents with suspicion and apprehension. Of the wretched circumstances of the Papal Court they reported that the Pope lay in an old palace of the Bishops of Orvieto, ruinous and decayed: When they came to his privy bedchamber, they passed three chambers "all naked and unhanged, the roofs fallen down, and, as we can guess, thirty persons, riff-raff and other, standing in the chamber for garnishment. As for the Pope's bedchamber, all the apparel in it was not worth twenty nobles, bed and all."[14]

The beleaguered Pope, made nearly frantic by his intolerable position, listened to the arguments of the Englishmen and well understood the implied threats. He tried to explain his own position. He was reminded of his supreme authority and the infallibility of his office. Seeking to avoid the persuasion of the Englishmen, Clement brought in two of his Cardinal advisers, Santi Quatro and Monte. Both were against the idea of a trial being held in England. In return the Englishmen protested that the necessary witnesses, and indeed the principals, could not be brought to Italy. In the end Clement was forced to a not very creditable compromise. He consented that a Commission to examine the facts of the case should be held in England, presided over by the Cardinals Wolsey and Campeggio. The latter, as the Pope's representative, would carry a document issued by the Pope, and if Henry's marriage were found to be invalid, Campeggio, with the authority of this document, a Decretal Bull, would pronounce Henry free to marry again. Gardiner and Fox thought that they had won a victory, for in England a trial would surely go the King's way, but the Pope was following an odious and shifting policy. Campeggio was instructed to take as much time as he could on the long journey to England. After his arrival he might show the Decretal Bull to the King, but he was never to allow it to leave his hands.

The Commission was projected in April of 1528, but Campeggio did not set foot in England until October. Even then he procrastinated so much that the trial did not commence until June of the following year. Wolsey knew what these delaying measures meant and fretted with anxiety, although at this point he apparently still enjoyed the favour and confidence of his master. Even Anne Boleyn was writing him kind and grateful letters. ". . . all the days of my life I am most bound, of all creatures, next the King's Grace, to love and serve your Grace: of the which, I beseech you, never to doubt, that ever I shall vary from this thought as long as any breath is in my body . . . And, as for the coming of the legate, I desire that much, and, if it be God's pleasure, I pray him to send this matter shortly to a good end; and then I trust, my Lord, to recompence part of your great pains."[15]

12

THE Queen was summoned to the great Hall of the Black Friar's Convent in London. The King, on a raised platform, sat at the upper end. Some distance away Catherine was given her place. The Cardinals, sitting lower than the King, flanked the royal presence, and near them the Archbishop of Canterbury and the Bishops were given position. Doctor Samson, afterwards Bishop of Chichester, and Doctor Bell, afterwards Bishop of Worcester, led those who pleaded for the King. Representing the Queen was John Fisher, Bishop of Rochester, and Doctor Standish, a Gray Friar and Bishop of St. Asaph.

The Papal Legate, racked with the gout, reported back to Rome every detail of the "whole tragic wretchedness of the subject." In cipher he wrote: "So far as I can see this passion of the King's is a most extraordinary thing. He sees nothing, he thinks of nothing but his Anne; he cannot be without her for an hour, and it moves one to pity to see how the King's life, the stability and downfall of the whole country, hang upon this one question . . . In the house of a foreigner, one cannot do all one wishes; the case has no defence. The King, especially in his own house, has no lack of procurators, attorneys, witnesses, and even laity who are hankering after his grace and favour. The Bishops of Rochester and St. Asaph have spoken and written in support of the marriage, also some men of learning have done the same, but in fear and on their own responsibility: no one comes forward any longer in the Queen's name."[1] He was wrong. John Fisher, the Bishop of Rochester, never ceased to champion the cause of the unhappy Catherine with unwavering courage.

Catherine had refused to admit the authority of the Court; nevertheless, on these first days she attended the trial. Dramatic was her response to the summons, "Catherine, Queen of England, come into the court." Slowly making her way past the prelates and dignitaries she knelt before her husband.

"Sir," she said, in a voice that all could hear, "I beseech you for all the loves that hath been between us, and for the love of God, let me have justice and right, take of me some pity and compassion, for I am a poor woman, and a stranger, born out of your Dominion. I have here no assured friend and much less indifferent counsel; I flee to you as to the head of justice within this realm . . . I take God and all the world to witness, that I have been to you a true, humble and obedient wife, ever conformable to your will and pleasure . . . being always well pleased and contented with all things wherein you had any delight or dalliance, whether it were in little or much . . . I loved all those whom ye loved only for your sake, whether I had cause or no; and whether they were my friends or my enemies. This twenty years I have been your true wife or more, and by me ye have had divers children, although it hath pleased God to call them out of this world, which hath been no default in me. And when ye had me at the first, I take God to be my judge, I was a true maid without touch of man; and whether it be true or no, I put it to your conscience."

What were the thoughts of Henry as he listened? The fortune that comes from truth? The justification that follows wrong? No man is completely villain. At this moment surely Henry was sick at heart. Surely at this critical time, there must have been, even for a fleeting moment, the accusation of conscience, the pain of doubt. He made no answer, nor did he speak any word when she concluded: "To God I commit my cause." She made a curtsy to her husband and then, with head held high, walked from the court.

The crier, under command, sought to bring her back. "Madam," he said, "ye be called again."

"It maketh no matter," was the brave answer, "for it is no indifferent court for me. Therefore, I will not tarry."[2] The mood of court, prejudiced of necessity, was heavy with sympathy for the Queen.

Henry made a bid to twist that sympathy to his own end. "She hath been to me as true," he said, "as obedient, and as conformable a wife, as I could in my fantasy wish or desire. She hath all the virtuous qualities that ought to be in a woman of her dignity, or in any other of baser estate . . ."

Cardinal Wolsey then asked the King to declare that he had not instigated the proceedings against Catherine. Henry readily absolved the Cardinal of all guilt and placed the blame on his conscience. The death of his children by Catherine and the lack of a male heir convinced him that he was being punished by God. "It drove me at last to consider the estate of this realm . . . whether I might take another wife . . . not for any carnal concupiscence, not for any displeasure or mislike of the Queen's person or age, with whom I could be as well content to continue during my life, if our marriage may stand with God's laws, as with any woman alive . . ." Again he lingered long upon his conscience, his wounded and ready conscience, and pleaded his cause with seeming humility and sincerity. His Bishops listened with docility, and their spokesman, the old Archbishop Warham, gave their answer. "That is true, if it pleases Your Highness. I doubt not that all my brethren here present will affirm the same."

There was a sudden stir in that packed room as plans went awry. John Fisher's voice rang throughout the room: "No, Sir, not I. Ye have not my consent thereto."

All eyes turned upon Fisher. The King was the first to speak: "Look here upon this"; he held the paper up. "Is not this your hand and seal?" Fisher looked angrily at his peers and then defiantly addressed the King: "No, forsooth, Sire, it is not my hand nor seal!"

Hastily Warham turned to Fisher. There was discreet murmuring on his part but the sturdy voice of Fisher rose high and with insistence: "I said to you, that I never would consent to no such an act, for it were against my conscience . . ."

The old Archbishop was all of a flutter, and in a flurry of words he tried to explain a forgery and said that he had thought that he had the power to affix the seal of Fisher. Steadily Fisher made reply: "Under your correction, my Lord, there is no thing more untrue."

Henry frowned and intruded: "Well, well," he said bluntly, "it shall make no matter. We will not stand with you in argument therein, for you are but one man."[3]

The case went on. The Queen refused to appear again and was declared contumacious. The King's will dominated the court, yet the proceedings were held to a tedious pace. Wolsey was for hurrying; Campeggio, the Italian, delayed. Forty witnesses were called, all acting for the one side. Fisher's voice was the only plea heard for Catherine. "Whom God hath joined together let no man put asunder," he thundered.

Wolsey listened with anxiety, for he knew well that this trial was in reality his trial, a test of his influence and strength. As it was, things were going far too slowly for the King. The Cardinal was summoned, and on his return from the royal presence, he met the Bishop of Carlyle. "Sir," said the latter, "it's a very hot day." "Yes," said Wolsey, "and if you had been as well chafed as I have been within this hour, you would say it were very hot."[4]

In desperation, he persuaded his fellow cardinal, Campeggio, to go with him to the Queen and make a final effort to change her thinking. She received them courteously

ANN BOLEYN

making apology for being engaged in the disorder and
paraphernalia of sewing. Her ladies stood about her.

"If it please you, to go into your private chamber," Wolsey said, "we will show you the cause of our coming."

"My Lord," she said calmly, "if you have anything to
say, speak it openly before all these folks; for I fear nothing
that you can say or allege against me, but that I would all
the world should both hear and see . . ."

Again the Cardinal looked at the circle of ladies-in-
waiting, all sympathetic to their mistress, all hostile to him.
He tried another stratagem and began to speak in Latin,
which he knew she well understood. But he was interrupted.

"Nay, good my Lord," Catherine said, "speak to me in
English I beseech you; although I understand Latin."

"We come both to know your mind . . ." declared Wolsey, "and also to declare secretly our opinions and our
counsel to you, which we have intended of very zeal and
obedience . . . to your Grace."

She thanked him. "But to make answer to your request
I cannot so suddenly, for I was set among my maidens at
work, thinking full little of any such matter, wherein there
needeth a longer deliberation . . . I had need of good counsel . . . think you . . . my lords, will any Englishmen counsel
or be friendly unto me against the King's pleasure, they
being his subjects? Nay, forsooth, my lords! I am destitute
and barren of friendship and counsel here in a foreign
region: and as for your counsel, I will not refuse but be
glad to hear."[5]

Relenting, she allowed them to talk to her in private.
They submitted their arguments as to her submission to the

King's will. But she was obstinate and remained unchanged, acting with the strength of one who was carrying the banner of right against wrong, acting with the immeasurable strength of a mother fighting for her child. Her daughter was the King's daughter, ánd unless she, the Queen, had a son by him, or unless death removed her from the scene, Mary was heiress to England's crown.

Clearly there was no hope of compromise. The trial dragged on, day by day, until finally Campeggio adjourned the court and transferred the case to Rome. It was as though a cannon had been exploded. Speechless with fury, Henry abandoned all pretense of civility and rushed from the Hall. His brother-in-law, Suffolk, acted for him: "It was never merry in England whilst we had cardinals amongst us!" As he spoke, he beat the table and glared at the two members of the Sacred College.

For a moment Wolsey, amidst all his anxieties, recovered some of his former dignity. He had once shielded Suffolk from Henry's displeasure.

When the King's sister had become the widow of King Louis of France she had, in secret and in haste, married Suffolk, who was in France to negotiate with her husband's successor. Suffolk had then sought Wolsey's help, explaining ungallantly that the Queen would not let him rest till he had granted her marriage, he having lain with her so much he feared she was with child. When Henry heard the news his anger had flared, but Wolsey had intervened, and had made smooth the way of the anxious bride and still more anxious groom. At that time the latter had written to the Cardinal that he was obliged to him next God and his master.

And now here they were, Duke and Cardinal, debtor and indebted. The Cardinal measured his words and faced the angry nobleman.

"Sir," he answered, "of all men within this realm, ye have the least cause to dispraise or be offended with cardinals: for if I, simple cardinal, had not been, you should have had at this present no head upon your shoulders . . ."[6]

It was an angry and frustrated Henry who went to Waltham Abbey to give the bitter news to Anne Boleyn. There was little hope for an annulment. If and when the court were to be reconvened, it would be in Rome. And in the Eternal City, the Pope made peace with Catherine's nephew, the Emperor Charles.

But to lighten the dejection of the royal lover, another hope came from Cambridge University. The future Archbishop of Canterbury, Thomas Cranmer, in a bid for Henry's favour, reasoned that since the whole matter hinged on an interpretation of the Scriptures, the case should be presented to biblical scholars. But not merely to the selectees of an ecclesiastical court. It was his suggestion that all the great universities of Christendom should be consulted. Henry, ever the ardent amateur theologian, took to the scheme with enthusiasm. Machinery was constructed and put into motion. Cambridge, and soon Oxford, voted for the King's cause. Royal messengers and English gold crossed the Channel. Poitiers was against him, and at Angers there was disagreement. The King of France intimidated the University of Paris into supporting Henry. Because of the same influence, Orleans, Bourges and Toulouse gave a similar verdict. But, perhaps because of Imperial pressure, Alcala and Salamanca opposed him, as did the University of Naples. Ferrara and Padua voted for the divorce and so would have the University of Vicenza, if the Bishop of that city had not intervened. A great deal of bribery accompanied these decisions, although in the Papal states the University of Bologna declared for the divorce and refused Henry's gold. Almost every available scholar of note was importuned; even eminent Jewish rabbis were engaged to endorse Henry's interpretation of Deuteronomy.

Cranmer's idea was to bring solid theological support to Henry, support that would influence the decision of Rome. But at this stage the Pope was not to be swayed. In fact, there was little courtesy now between England and Rome. When Campeggio left England his baggage was seized and searched, in violation of all recognized diplomatic custom. It was Henry's final attempt to secure the Decretal Bull.

The tragedy of Wolsey's downfall gained momentum. On Saturday, the 9th of October, even while presiding at his duties of Lord Chancellor, he was indicted. A week later he was ordered to give up the Great Seal. It was a momentous hour in England's story. The Papal Legate, he who represented the power and authority of the Church, was challenged by the secular power. That for which Becket had died was again at stake. Wolsey was not equal to the occasion. Instead of courageous defiance, instead of martyrdom, and perhaps victory, he chose to beg, hoping that past friendship between himself and Henry would stay his destruction.

The King was not insensitive to the bond that had existed between him and the Cardinal, but always there was the whisper of Anne Boleyn. "Is it not a marvelous thing," she

sked her lover one day, "to consider what debt and danger
he Cardinal hath brought you in with all his subjects?"

"How so, Sweetheart," asked the King. She talked of
he heavy taxes the Cardinal had brought on the people,
nd when the King tried to give justification she interrupted
with: "Nay, Sir, besides all that, what things hath he
wrought in this realm to your great slander and dishonour?
There was never a nobleman within this realm that if had
done but half as much he were well worthy to lose his head."

"Why I then perceive," Henry said, "ye are not the
Cardinal's friend."

"Forsooth, Sir," came the feminine answer, "I have no
cause, nor any other that loveth your Grace, no more hath
your Grace, if you consider well his doings."[7]

Following Campeggio's departure from England, the
King sent the dukes of Suffolk and Norfolk to Wolsey with
he request to surrender the Great Seal. The Cardinal was
incredulous, but when, on the following day, they returned
with the King's letters, he obeyed the royal command. The
Cardinal was stripped of his wealth and banished to his
country home at Esher. For a while it seemed as though
Henry might spare him any further hurt. But Wolsey had
too many enemies and too few friends, and relentless in the
effort to destroy him was the Boleyn faction, fearing that if
Henry weakened and the Cardinal came back to favour, the
King's "Great Matter" might be left to the direction of
Rome. He had been untrue to his responsibilities. Because
of his shameful subservience to Henry he had brought
grievous detriment to the Church. He had abused and
deserted the Legatine power. He had broken his priestly
vows. He had sought to secure the divorce by every device

at his command. All these things were true. But no man
believed that, if the dreaded time of decision arrived, Wolsey would permit the Church in England to abandon and
reject the authority of the Holy See.

When he departed from London, it was by barge, and a
noisy crowd gathered on the banks of the Thames hoping
that he would be taken to the Tower. They yelled a vigorous
disapproval when his craft did not land at the Traitors'
Gate.

Henry had a turn of heart at this moment. He sent a
messenger, Sir Harry Norris, who gave the Cardinal a
bejewelled ring and a message to be "of good cheer, for he
was as much in his Highness' favour as ever he was, and so
shall be."[8] Given some hope by this symbol of the King's
favour, the Cardinal proceeded to Esher. Here, in a country
house, his existence, if not literally, was actually that of a
prisoner, living with all the terrible uncertainties and fears
of a prisoner not yet sentenced. He who had ruled a kingdom with a heavy hand, who had insulted the powerful and
goaded the great, he who had fostered the whims of his
Prince and who had made, or at least helped make, a tyrant
was under no illusions as to how dark and cruel his fate
could be.

Henry, for a while, continued to send him messages and
marks of friendship. But Anne Boleyn's father, the Earl
of Wiltshire, and her uncle, the Duke of Norfolk, persisted
in their campaign to ruin him. Unwisely perhaps, he took
possession of his Archiepiscopal See of York and made
ready to be installed with some of the pomp of former days.
It was enough for his enemies. On the fourth of November,
the Earl of Northumberland, who, as a stripling, had been

chided by the Cardinal because of his passion for Anne Boleyn, burst in upon him with terrible words: "My Lord, I arrest you for high treason."

Under arrest Wolsey was ordered back to London. Unlike the citizens of that town, the crowds of York gathered around him crying, "God save your Grace, God save your Grace! The foul evil take all that have thus taken you from us! We pray God that a very vengeance may light upon them."

So unpopular was his arrest in those regions that his guards were obliged to travel in the night. Dark and gloomy was the long journey, dark indeed for Wolsey with the knowledge that every mile brought him closer to the Tower. They rode in stages, stopping at Hardwick, then Nottingham, and by now it was obvious to every member of the little band that the Cardinal was not only ailing in spirit but also in health. On the third day of the journey, Saturday, November 26th, they arrived in the darkness of night at the Augustinian Abbey at Leicester. By torchlight the prisoner was escorted into the Abbey. The Abbot and monks stood in sad greeting. As he passed amongst them Wolsey said: "Father Abbot, I am come to lay my weary bones among you."

Once to his bed, the Cardinal never rose again. On Monday night he called the monks and told them that by the stroke of eight in the morning he would be dead. The pale dawn of the cold winter morning came, and the old man made a long and full confession to the Abbot. He talked for over a full hour, then, anxious for his charge, came the Keeper of the Tower, Sir William Kingston. The official asked him how he did. "Sir," answered the broken man,

"I tarry but the will and pleasure of God to render my simple soul into his divine hands."

Then came the sad words that were ever to be remembered: "If I had served God as diligently as I have done the king, he would not have given me over in my gray hairs."

He turned on what was his deathbed and further addressed Kingston: "This is the just reward that I must receive for my worldly diligence and pains that I have had to do him service; only to satisfy his main pleasure, not regarding my godly duty. Wherefore I pray you, with all my heart, to have me most kindly commended unto his Royal Majesty; beseeching him, in my behalf, to call to his most gracious remembrance all matters proceeding between him and me, from the beginning of the world unto this day, and the progress of the same, and most and chiefly in the weighty matter yet depending: then shall his conscience declare, whether I have offended him or no. He is sure a Prince of a royal courage, and hath a princely heart; and rather than he will either miss, or want any part of his will or appetite, he will put the loss of one half of his realm in danger."

The halting voice went on conjuring up the past. "For, I assure you, I have often kneeled before him in his Privy Chamber, on my knees for space of an hour or two, to persuade him from his will and appetite; but I could never bring to pass to dissuade him therefrom. Therefore, Master Kingston, if it chance hereafter you to be one of his Privy Counsel, as for your wisdom and other qualities ye are meet to be, I warn you to be well advised and assured what matter ye put in his head or ye shall never put it out again." After giving a strong warning concerning the heresies that were

eing imported into England, he realized it was nearing
e time that he said he would die.

"Master Kingston, farewell," he said, "I can no more,
ut wish all things to have good success. My time draweth
n fast. I may not tarry with you. And forget not, I pray
ou, what I have said and charged you withall; for, when
am dead, ye shall, peradventure, remember my words
uch better."[9]

He called for the Father Abbot. He was anointed with
e Holy Oil and all the solemn rites of the Last Sacrament
ere performed.

As the Abbot concluded his functions the great bells of
e Abbey tolled the hour. It was eight o'clock. And before
e eighth 'stroke came, Cardinal Wolsey was dead. His
orpse was dressed in the full splendour of his rank, the
mbroidered mitre placed on his head, the ring on his finger.
efore the coffin was closed, the Mayor of Leicester and
ther notables were called to take a last look at him so that
here would be no suspicion or murmur as to his death. The
offin was then carried into the Lady Chapel, where all that
ay it was guarded and all the next night. Then, in the
orning, the monks sang the Requiem for his soul.

The remains of Cardinal Wolsey were committed to the
arth, but he who had loved pomp and palaces so much was
iven no high monument to mark his tomb. And to this day
he place of his burial is not known.

13

WHEN the Great Seal had been surrendered b
Wolsey there arose the question as to who woul
be his successor. According to Erasmus, ther
were many around the King who wished to reappoint Arch
bishop Warham but he refused because of his age. It i
difficult to accept Erasmus' opinion because it is quite cer
tain that the Dukes of Norfolk and Suffolk, and indeed th
entire Boleyn faction, would not, at this critical time
permit the Chancellorship to be entrusted to an ecclesiastic
Who was to take Wolsey's place?

There was a scholar renowned throughout Christendom
The same man was a skilled lawyer. He had been a suc
cessful ambassador. Perhaps of equal or greater importance
he was not over-ambitious or self-seeking. Churchme

verywhere respected him for his piety and theology, yet
e had been outspoken in his criticism of clerical abuses;
 factor of high value to a regime that, under the pretence
f reform, was to curb prelatical power.

The tempest that had struck Wolsey now swirled Thomas
More to the highest office of the realm. On the twenty-fifth
of October he was summoned to Greenwich, where the
King gave him the Great Seal and proclaimed him Lord
Chancellor of England. He was the first commoner and
layman not possessed of high judicial experience to be so
honoured.

In order that his dignity might not appear mean after
the grandiose affectations of Wolsey, the Duke of Norfolk
provided a pageant for his installation. A long procession
of nobles and judges and professors of law preceded the
new Chancellor to Westminster Hall. Having placed More
on the high judgment seat, the Duke, speaking for the King,
gave him eulogy.

There was no objection to the appointment from any
quarter, only applause. Even Wolsey, from his place of
exile, stated that the best choice had been made. Friendship
did not prompt the compliment. The only bond between the
two was a common service to the Crown.

The new Spanish Ambassador, Chapuys, had just landed
on English soil. Representing Catherine's nephew, he could
hardly be expected to view with friendly eyes any action
that was instigated by the group that now had the King's
ear, yet he wrote back to the Emperor Charles: "The Chancellor's seal . . . has continued in the hands of the Duke
of Norfolk till this morning, when it was delivered to
Sir Thomas More. Everyone is delighted at his promotion,

because he is an upright and learned man and a good servant of the Queen."[1]

More opened the Parliament which had as its first important business the impeachment of his predecessor. The King was there to listen. It has been charged that on this occasion More spoke harshly and without chivalry. It must be remembered, however, that the rhetorical phraseology of the day differed from modern usage. He spoke under the obligation of duty, not for himself, but for his Royal Master, and it was his own opinion that the whole grievous business of Henry's divorce would never have come into being if the Cardinal had not held out some hope to the King.

The usual compliments were paid to Henry. More likened him to "a good shepherd which not only keepeth and attendeth well his sheep, but also foreseeth and provideth for all thing, which either may be hurtful or noisome to his flock, or may preserve and defend the same against all perils that may chance to come, so the King, which was the shepherd, ruler and governor of this realm, vigilantly foreseeing things to come, considered how divers laws were now made by long continuance of time and mutation of things, very insufficient and imperfect: and also by the frail condition of man, divers new enormities were sprung amongst the people, for the which no law was made to reform the same which was the very cause why at that time, the King had summoned his High Court of Parliament . . . If a prince is compared to his riches, he is but a rich man; if . . . to his honour, he is but an honourable man; but compare him to the multitude of his people and the number of his flock, then he is a ruler, a governor of might and puissance; so

hat his people maketh him a prince, as of the multitude of
heep, cometh the name of shepherd: and as you see that
mongst a great flock of sheep some be rotten and faulty,
which the good shepherd sendeth from the good sheep, so
he great wether which is of late fallen, as you all know . . .
uggled with the king, that all men must needs guess and
hink that he thought in himself that the king had no wit to
perceive his crafty doing, or else that he presumed that the
ing would not see nor know his fraudulent juggling and
ttempts: but he was deceived, for his Grace's sight was so
quick and penetrable, that he saw him, yea and through
him, both within and without, so that all thing to him was
pen, and according to his desert he hath had a gentle
orrection, which small punishment the king will not to be
n example to other offenders, but clearly declareth that
whosoever hereafter shall make like attempt to commit like
offense, shall not escape with like punishment . . ." [2]

The Bill of Attainder projected against Wolsey was preceded by ferocious and often ridiculous charges. It was
alleged that Wolsey had been possessed of an evil disease
and had breathed it "upon your most Noble Grace with his
perilous and infective breath." He had said, and written in
divers letters "the King and I." He had forced a gentleman
to marry his mistress, the mother of his two children. And
so the list of crimes went on. More could not have been
happy in reciting the unsavoury charges. But it was his duty
as the King's mouthpiece to tell the Commons the mood of
the Sovereign, and duty was a binding obligation to this
man who rigidly accepted his anointed King as one possessed of authority under God.

He knew the dangers that were ahead, yet it was with

apparent calm that he faced them. This Parliament which he addressed was, under the goad of Henry, to make more drastic changes than any which had ever happened before in the history of English legislation. In seven years England was to break with Rome. The Royal supremacy over the English Church was to become law. The monasteries were to be looted and their wealth scattered in a manner that exceeded anything of the kind since William the Conqueror had landed. The power of the Crown was to rise to a strength which it never had before. New laws were to be made which created such grave social problems that an economic revolution was effected. It was not a Parliament as we understand that body to be in modern times. It represented the rich and the privileged, the great landowners, the powerful merchants, rather than the people. It represented those who envied the monastic landlords and who resented the wide influence of the clergy. It was a Parliament that was not only creature to the King but in full sympathy with his ambitions. Fear and greed made for a happy partnership on this occasion. Schism with Rome presented a dazzling prospect of rich spoils to be divided amongst those who were possessed of Henry's good will. Those close to him, as Cardinal Pole, his cousin, pointed out, did not conceal their desire to abolish Papal power, to despoil the monks, and exalt the Monarch at the expense of the Church.

More probably hoped that if he could not act as a deterrent to the King's passion, the Pope might give the annulment, or that Henry, in time, would tire of his mistress.

In the scale of precedence the Lord Chancellor came before the Dukes of Norfolk and Suffolk and the Archbishops. At public ceremonies there was on his right a golden scepter surmounted by the Royal Crown, as a sign of his power under the King, and on his left a book as a sign of his knowledge of the law; the Royal Seal carried before him. These magnificences caused him to remark with a smile that when men bared their heads before him it did not keep his head as warm as his own hat.

His father, Sir John More, was now nearly ninety years old, but well in health and mind. He had been appointed to and was performing the duties of a judge in the Court of King's Bench. Every time Thomas More proceeded to his own Court, he would first go into the Court of King's Bench and kneel before his parent and ask for his blessing.

Such humility was often misunderstood. The Duke of Norfolk, paying a call upon him one day, found him in church singing with the choir and dressed like them in a simple surplice.

"God body! god body!" said the outraged Duke. "My Lord Chancellor a parish clerk! A parish clerk! You dishonour the King and his Office."

"No," answered More, "your Grace may not think that the King, your master and mine, will with me, for serving of God, his master, be offended, or thereby account his office dishonoured."[3]

The new Chancellor made it known that he would hold his Court between eight and eleven in the morning, then, after the noon meal, he would sit with open door and listen to all who chose to present their cases to him, examining their petitions and giving judgment according to law and conscience. He was determined that the law should be administered not only with justice but without senseless delay.

One of his sons-in-law complained that when Cardinal
Wolsey was Lord Chancellor, not only the members of his
privy Chamber, but his doorkeepers as well, got great gain
by him. Since he had married one of More's daughters, he
might of reason look for some commodity; but More was
so ready to do for every poor man, and keep no doors shut
from them, that he could find no gains at all, which was a
great discouragement, and all the more so because if he
should take anything from his own friends, for bringing
them into More's presence, he "should do them great wrong
for that they might do as much for themselves as he could
do for them; which condition although he thought in Sir
Thomas More very commendable, to him, being his son, he
found it nothing profitable."

"You say well, Son," answered More, "I do not mislike
that you are of conscience so scrupulous; but many other
ways be there, Son, that I may both do yourself good, and
pleasure your friend also. For some time, may I by my word
stand your friend instead; and sometime I may by my letter
help him; or if he have a cause depending before me, at
your request I may hear him before another. Or if his cause
be not all the best, yet may I move the parties to fall to
some reasonable end by arbitrament. Howbeit this one
thing, Son, I assure thee on my faith, that if the parties
will at my hands call for justice, then, although it were my
father stood on the one side, and the devil on the other,
his cause being good, the devil should have right."[4]

When More came to the Chancellor's Court he found
there was much to do. Many cases there were that had
dragged on for twenty years. With tremendous industry he
set out to remedy the situation and, within a few terms, he

heard each cause as it was made ready for hearing. There came one welcome morning when he was informed by the officers of the court that there was no more unfinished business, not another cause or petition to be put before him. So was born a popular rhyme:[5]

> *When MORE some time had Chancellor been,*
> *No more suits did remain;*
> *The same shall never more be seen*
> *Till MORE be there again.*

His reputation for justice and honesty as a magistrate was to become a tradition, yet, oddly enough, in the records that remain there is no mention of any important judgment or major legal decision made by him.

One afternoon, in his great open hall, he rendered an opinion worthy of Solomon. A beggar woman appeared before him and complained that her little dog had been stolen from her and was now in the possession of the Lord Chancellor's wife. She had tried to get it back but had been put off by Sir Thomas' serving men. More listened to her story, then summoned his wife. He bade her stand at the upper end of the hall, then he ordered the beggar woman to take her place at the opposite end. He took the dog in his arms and stood between the two women, and bade each of them to call the dog.

"Are you content," he asked, "that I shall decide this controversy that is between you concerning this dog?"

On their answering in the affirmative, he commanded: "Each of you call the dog by his name, and to whom the dog cometh, she shall have it."

Both women made their cries. The dog, not intimidated by rank, ran to the poor woman. Whereupon More gave the judgment in her favour, and along with it a gold coin. So overcome was the beggar by his justice and liberality that she promptly made a present of the animal to Lady More.[6]

Wolsey had often interfered with the Courts of common law, and More believed that many changes should be made in the mode of procedure. He granted injunctions and supported them with firmness when necessary. The common law judges, fixed in their ways, were not happy when their proceedings were examined and their verdicts over-ridden. There was considerable grumbling, which More met in typical fashion. He ordered Master Crooke, chief of the Six Clerks, to make a docket containing the whole number and causes of all such injunctions, as either in his time had already passed, or that at present depended in any of the King's Courts at Westminster before him. This done, he invited all the Judges to dine with him in the Council Chamber at Westminster. After dinner, he rehearsed the complaints brought to him against his injunctions. These he refuted one by one, moreover assured them both the number and causes of every one of them, "in order so plainly, that upon full debating of those matters, they were all enforced to confess that they, in like case, could have done no otherwise themselves."[7]

He also reminded them that if the Justices of every Court would themselves mitigate and reform the rigour of the law there should be no more injunctions granted by him.

When his guests displayed no great enthusiasm for his

unwelcome advice, he warned them that he would continue to issue injunctions just as long as they persisted in their present practices and actions. The dinner ended on a somewhat sour note, and afterwards the Chancellor confided to his son-in-law that in his opinion the Judges had no wish to accept responsibility or follow principle. "I perceive, Son, why they like not so to do. For they see that they may, by the verdict of the Jury, cast off all quarrels from themselves upon them, which they account their chief defense, and therefore am I compelled to abide the adventure of all such reports."[8]

Accusations have been made and have lingered, that More was unfair and cruel to those accused of heresy. Nothing could be less true. That he led in the fight against heresy is quite true. In 1519 when Henry made it his business to extirpate the Lutheran heresy, More helped the King revise his book against Luther. Later, in 1532, he assumed leadership in the controversy. But it was not until he had resigned the Chancellorship that heresy was made high treason, punishable by death. It should be remembered that during all the years of More's influence at Court not a single heretic was sentenced to death in London. The burnings did not commence until after the clergy had conferred on Henry the title of Supreme Head.

There were two cases in which More ordered floggings. One was a boy whom he had taken into his household and who insisted on spreading his propaganda and teaching another child his heresies. More ordered him to be whipped, not for his beliefs, but for his persistence in propagandizing. The second person to receive the lash was punished for his conduct in church. At the solemn moment of the Elevation, this misguided creature made a habit of creeping up behind women who were praying and throwing their skirts above their ears!

It is inconceivable that the gentle author of *Utopia* should resort to torture as a weapon against heresy. Kindness and reason constituted the method which he used against Lutheranism. If he failed to convert by these measures, he was content that the recipients of his arguments should not spread their errors. He invited a German scholar, one Grinaeus, who was a professed Lutheran, to be a guest in his house. Years later, after More's death, Grinaeus dedicated a book to More's son, John. He wrote: "Your father at that time held the highest rank, but apart from that, by his many excellent qualities, he was clearly marked out as the chief man in the realm, whilst I was obscure and unknown. Yet, for the love of learning, in the midst of public and private business, he found time to converse much with me: he, the Chancellor of the Kingdom, made me sit at his table; going to and from the Court he took me with him and kept me ever by his side. He had no difficulty in seeing that my religious opinions were on many points different from his own, but his goodness and courtesy were unchanged. Though he differed so much from my views, yet he helped us in word and deed and carried through my business at his own expense. He gave us a young man of considerable literary attainments, John Harris, to accompany us on our journey, and to the authorities of the University of Oxford he sent a letter, couched in such terms, that at once, not only were the libraries of all the colleges thrown open to us, but the students, as if they had been touched by the rod of Mercury, showed us the greatest favour . . . I returned to my country overjoyed at the treasures I had discovered, laden with your father's generous gifts, and almost overwhelmed by his kindness."[9]

14

THE sorry mess and confusion born of the King's infatuation, while giving sadness to many, provided opportunity for an unscrupulous, clever and ambitious man who was rapidly assuming a role of importance at the Court. Thomas Cromwell, former agent of Wolsey, had transferred his services to Henry, and such was his talent that he climbed fast, securing the confidence of the King and earning the dubious distinction of being named as the real author of the English Reformation. He was a shadowy figure, emerging from the shadows, and utilizing shadows throughout his devious career. Without formal education, without influential friends, without money, he had made his own way, until he could now whisper schemes in the Royal ear. He was the son of a small tavern keeper in Putney. In his youth, as a military vagabond, he had wandered to Italy. There he learned the language and there he read Machiavelli, whose disciple he was to remain all his life. Somehow, he managed to accumulate some money on the shores of the Mediterranean, and there branched out as a money-lender. Plying this occupation, he learned something of the law, and on his return to his native land, he managed to insinuate himself into the service of Wolsey. When the Cardinal suppressed some of the smaller monasteries in order to use their revenues for his great new college at Oxford, Cromwell was the instrument that he used. The wily man of business did his work well. He set a pattern that would one day result in the gigantic robbery of all the monasterial establishments in England.

From the very beginning, Cromwell was unpopular at the Court, but little he cared, seeking only to win the King's favour. On meeting him one day, Thomas More offered him some advice: "Master Cromwell, you are now entered into the service of a most noble, wise and liberal Prince; if you wi'l follow my poor advice, you shall, in your counsel giving unto his grace, ever tell him what he ought to do, but never tell him what he is able to do; so shall you show yourself a true faithful servant and a right worthy councillor. For if a Lion knew his own strength, hard were it for any man to rule him."[1]

Perhaps Cromwell remembered More's warning when in after years Henry was to send him in his turn to the scaffold, but at this stage he was confident of his abilities to guide and control the King. His targets included divorce, schism, and possession of the Church's property in England. Eventually he lost his head, but not before he had succeeded in his ambition. He was able to endow his nephew, also a tavern keeper's son, with no less than thirteen monastic estates. This man's son built his major residence upon the ruins of a nunnery, and his grandson was Oliver Cromwell.

Since Henry's attempts to cast aside his wife were becoming increasingly unpopular throughout England he made, in the spring of 1530, a new effort to secure the approval of the Pope. With a glaring lack of tact he appointed as emissary Anne Boleyn's father, the newly created Earl of Wiltshire. At Bologna, the Englishman met with both Pope and Emperor, and while he made a great pretence of talking about peace amongst European nations and an alliance against the Turks, he brazenly opened up the business of the divorce. It was only natural that he should have no success with the Emperor. The Pope was equally emphatic. In fact, he made use of Wiltshire's presence to summon Henry to come to Rome and appear before the Rota.

Meanwhile Cranmer's plan concerning the opinions of the universities, was bearing fruit. The replies, many of them favourable, most of them subsidized, were coming in, and Henry decided they should be presented at a meeting of Parliament. Thus the Lord Chancellor, in fulfillment of his duties, was forced to lead twelve spiritual and temporal Peers to the House of Commons, and there to deliver the following address:

"You, of this worshipful House, I am sure be not so ignorant, but you know well that the King, our Sovereign Lord, hath married his brother's wife; for she was both wedded and bedded by his brother Prince Arthur, and therefore you may surely say that he hath married his brother's wife if this marriage be good—as so many clerks do doubt. Wherefore the King, like a virtuous Prince willing to be satisfied in his conscience, and also for the surety of his realm, hath with great deliberation consulted with great clerks, and hath sent my Lord of London here present to the chief Universities of all Christendom, to know their opinions and judgment in that behalf. And although the universities of Oxford and Cambridge had been sufficient to discuss the cause, yet they being in his realm, and to avoid all suspicion of partiality, he hath sent into the realm of France, Italy, the Pope's dominions, and the Venetians, to know their judgment in that behalf, which have concluded, written and sealed their determinations according as you shall hear read."

Sir Brian Tuke opened the box and read aloud the opinions, all favourable to Henry. Again the Lord Chancellor spoke: "Now you of this Common House may report in your countries what you have seen and heard and then all men shall perceive that the King hath not attempted this matter of will or pleasure as some strangers report, but only for the discharge of his conscience, and the security of the succession of his realm. This is the cause of our repair hither to you, and now we will depart."[2]

The dilemma was becoming increasingly difficult for More. He confided in no one, going about his business, but the words of Christ must have haunted him: "Render therefore to Caesar the things that are Caesar's; and to God, the things that are God's."

The issues involved were not so clear as they seem today. Many learned and good men were in all sincerity for the King's cause. And, too, there was the magnetic charm and undeniable authority of the consecrated person of the Monarch who, after prorogation of Parliament, pressed More for his private opinion. On one of these occasions the Lord Chancellor fell on his knees and begged Henry to revive in his memory the admonishment he had given More on the day he had bestowed the Great Seal: "First look upon God, and after God upon me."

As yet the Pope had given no absolute or final decision. Procrastination was the Papal policy. Clement had wanted to placate the powerful English sovereign. Was not Henry the Defender of the Faith? Besides, the Emperor had asked no more than justice. So he had entertained Henry's petition, then hesitated, and finally professed his inability to conclude the matter. Henry became impatient and sent a violent message to the Pope accusing him of being a servant of the Emperor. Soon after, Clement, in a Papal Brief, renewed a previous Edict and threatened ecclesiastical punishment for Henry and any woman who should attempt wedlock with him while the case was in the hands of the Rota. After the issuance of this Brief there was little hope in Henry's mind that he could force the Pope to his wishes. Urged by Cromwell, he now undertook the first major and drastic move in the separation of England and the Holy See. A general Convocation of the English clergy was called and the dread charge of *praemunire* was hurled at them, the same accusation that had destroyed Wolsey. In acknowledging his legatine authority, they too, it was charged, had been guilty of treason. Papal jurisdiction had trespassed upon the sovereignty of England.

The air was heavy with intimidation and threat. Submissive and terrified, the clergy volunteered to pay a fine of 160,000 crowns. The King rejected the offer. They advanced the tribute by another 400,000 crowns. Again they

were refused, unless, with the money, they would accept
him as the Supreme Head of the Church. Timid though
they were, and even though they owed their benefices and
appointments to him, the clergy made no haste to grant
what was almost a command. For three sessions they pondered. To give in to the King would surrender that which
St. Thomas à Becket had died for, freedom of the Church
from secular control. Courageous John Fisher gave warning and voiced his defiance, but finally suggested that the
King could have the title providing the words were added,
"so far as law of God allows." The Archbishop of Canterbury, weak in his old age and desperately striving for con-
ciliation, then said that it would not be in error to salute
the King as "their singular protector, only and Supreme
Lord, and so far as the law of Christ allows, even Supreme
Head."[3] There was a great silence at his suggestion, and the
Archbishop tremulously stated that "as silence signified consent, the new title should become fact."

"It is not intended to infringe the authority of the Pope,"
declared Henry, "provided His Holiness will pay due regard
to me; otherwise I know what to do."

His Queen had an answer for him. "The Pope," she said,
"is the only true sovereign and vicar of God who has power
to judge of spiritual matters of which marriage is one."

With Cranmer to assist, Henry now exercised his own
brand of theology. "If a man be excommunicated because
he doth that is good, or will not do that is ill, the sentence
of excommunication is none . . . The Church of God hath
its foundation set upon a firm and steadfast stone of truth
through faith, and not upon the mutable and wilful pleasure
of Peter's successors."[4]

The silence of the Lord Chancellor could only have one meaning and was highly dangerous at this anxious time. The alert Spanish Ambassador wrote to the Emperor that More was in danger of being dismissed from the Chancellorship and that when Henry had forced the clergy to acknowledge him as Supreme Head of the English Church, More had wished to resign. Grateful that England's Lord Chancellor was in sympathy with Catherine, Charles sent a letter to him in care of the Spanish Ambassador. But More, ever loyal to his conscience and to his office, refused to accept the letter and told the Ambassador that if the letter were given him, he must pass it on to his Sovereign.

It was on the thirteenth day of July, 1530, that Henry dropped every pretence and left his wife for all time. As far as he was concerned, she was not his wife nor his Queen any longer. If Rome continued to be stubborn and would not grant the divorce, then his own Church would oblige. But his purpose was so unpopular that he realized that he would have to proceed slowly, and as was his usual tactic, he utilized the instrument of mock legality to which was added a voluble and hypocritical piety.

When Anne Boleyn openly was installed in the apartments formerly belonging to Catherine, the Pope sent a Brief to Henry, deploring his conduct, and asking him to stay away from Anne Boleyn until a decision had been given by the Rota. The Brief had no effect upon the King's actions. Instead it provoked another attack upon the English clergy. "We thought that the clergy of our realm had been our subjects wholly," he declared, "but now we have well perceived that they be but half our subjects—yea, and scarce our subjects. For all the Prelates at their consecration, make an oath to the Pope, clean contrary to the oath that they make to us, so that they seem to be his subjects and not ours, the copy of both the oaths, I deliver here to you, requiring you to invent some order, that we be not thus deluded, of our Spiritual subjects."[5]

Parliament was uneasy. Already a deputation of members had asked for a dissolution. But Henry had further business for them. Following a plan conceived by Cromwell, the Commons, in the form of a supplication, complained of clerical abuses and begged for reform. Chapuys wrote the emperor that "Churchmen will be of less account than shoemakers, who have the power of assembling and making their own statutes. The King also wishes bishops not to lay hands on persons accused of heresy. . . . The Chancellor and the Bishops oppose him. He is very angry, especially with the Chancellor and the Bishop of Winchester . . ."[6]

When the complaints of the Commons had been given to the clergy, Cromwell's scheme advanced to its next stage. He requested Parliament to abolish annates, the payment of his first year's revenue that was made to the Holy See by each newly appointed Bishop. There was such an unexpected resistance to the passing of this bill that the King came in person to observe the final vote. Needless to say, in his formidable presence, the act was passed. No more annates were to be sent to Rome unless at the King's pleasure. The Papal Nuncio was informed of Parliament's action, but it was also hinted to him that the payments would be commenced again if a proper understanding could be arrived at between His Holiness and the King.

There were several incidents at this time to give evidence

of the general discontent. An angry mob hissed Anne Boleyn. Two Grey Friars of Greenwich delivered public sermons against the King. When one of these courageous monks was angrily told by a Court attendant that he should be sewed in a sack and thrown in the Thames, he gave the brave reply that "these threats are for courtiers. The way to Heaven is open as well by water as by land."

Parliament, smarting under the constant bullying of Henry, was addressed by More, who in his capacity as Lord Chancellor asked them to raise monies for troops to patrol the Scotch border. One member of the Commons named Temse bravely asserted that the danger was not with the Scots and that Henry should be asked to live with his rightful wife so that her nephew, who ruled both Spain and the Low Countries, would not be incited to enmity. The motion of Temse was carried with enthusiasm.

The unhappy clergy sought to temporize and compromise, but to no avail. The King, applying relentless pressure and threatening mass punishment, was determined that they surrender completely. All resistance soon vanished. In abject panic, they signed a document known as "the Submission of the Clergy." It was well named, for in it the Clergy swore to make no move in any manner without the Royal assent. On May 15th, 1532, the Archbishop of Canterbury gave the document to Henry. The Church in England was now the property of the King. It was an historic event, the subjection of the Church to the temporal power.

The next day, Sir Thomas More surrendered his seals of office.

15

EVEN at this critical time, More employed his wit in giving the news to his family. They were at Mass. In his capacity as the King's first minister, More had conformed with practice and sat with his gentlemen in a special pew. At the conclusion of the devotions, one of these gentlemen would come to Lady More and inform her "Madame, my Lord is gone." On this day, unaccompanied by any attendants, it was Sir Thomas himself who came to his wife's pew, and, making a low bow, told her with unmistakable meaning, "Madame, my Lord is gone."[1] She was not pleased.

He left office a poor man, with but a remnant of his former wealth and no pension. There still lived about him the little commonwealth of his children and grandchildren that was his joy. These he now called together, and discussing with them the change of his fortunes explained that in all probability their mode and style of living would be altered. He sought to give them comfort and quite cheerfully told them: "I have been brought up at Oxford, at an Inn of Chancery, at Lincoln's Inn, and also in the King's Court, from the lowest degree to the highest; and yet have I, in yearly revenues at this present, left me little above an hundred pounds by the year; so that now must we hereafter if we like to live together, be contented to become contributaries together. But, by my counsel, it shall not be best for us to fall to the lowest fare first; we will not, therefore, descend to Oxford fare, nor to the fare of New Inn, but we will begin with the Lincoln's Inn diet, where many right worshipful and of good years, do live full well; which, if we find not ourselves the first year able to maintain, then will we the next year go one step down to New Inn fare, wherewith many an honest man is well contented. If that exceed our ability too, then will we next year after descend to Oxford fare, where many grave, learned, and ancient fathers be continually conversant; which, if our power stretch not to maintain neither, then may we yet, with bags and wallets go a begging together, and hoping that for pity some good folks will give us their charity, at every man's door to sing a *Salve Regina,* and so still keep company and be merry together."[2]

He could no longer afford the staff of officers and servants who had attended him as Lord Chancellor, but they were not abruptly discharged. One of his first concerns was to find employment for all. Various noblemen and bishops were prevailed upon to take into their service the higher ranking members of his entourage. His state barge, along

THOMAS CROMWELL

with its crew of eight, went to his successor, Lord Audley. That necessary appendage to the train of any great man of that day, his Jester, he recommended and gave to the Lord Mayor of London. The light-hearted clown had quipped, "Chancellor More is Chancellor no more." But he also had wept, and it was by force that he was conveyed to his new master.

More could not have had any illusions concerning the dark way that was ahead, but the resignation of the Chancellorship brought to him a temporary peace and happiness. In a letter to Erasmus he wrote that being free from public business he might have some time "to devote to God and myself, that, by the grace of a great and good God, and by the favour of an indulgent prince, I have at last obtained."[3]

Years before, when Warham had resigned the Chancellorship, More had congratulated him on retiring "from the affairs of the world and the bustle of courts . . . you will pass your time gently and peacefully in literature and philosophy."[4]

His health was not good, and apparently having no desire—or perhaps thinking it unseemly for an ex-Lord Chancellor—to resume practice of the law, he turned to his pen with an increasing industry. At last he could devote all his hours to that which was so close to his heart, a campaign to combat the spread of Lutheranism. As Lord Chancellor, he could have employed force, but he always preferred to use the weapons of logic and argument. Now there was the opportunity. To Erasmus he wrote: "Here are you in a condition which would break the spirit of a vigorous youth, still bringing out book after book, for the instruction and admiration of the world. What matter the

attacks upon you? No great writer ever escaped malig-
nity . . . You allow frankly that if you could have forseen
these pestilent heresies you would have been less outspoken
on certain points. Doubtless the Fathers, had they expected
such times as ours, would have been more cautious in their
utterances. They had their own disorders to attend to, and
did not think of the future . . . The Bishops and the King
tried to check these new documents, but they spread wonderfully. The teachers of them retreat into the Low Countries, as into a safe harbour, and send over their works
written in English. Our people read them, partly in thought-
lessness, partly from a malicious disposition. They enjoy
them, not because they think them true, but because they
wish them to be true . . ."⁵

The speed with which he moved his pen was amazing.
Unhampered by public duties, he completed his *Confutation
of Tyndale's Answer,* a letter against Frith, the *Apology,* a
work in defence of the clergy, *The Debellation of Salem and
Bizance,* and his *Answer to the book which a nameless
heretic hath named The Supper of the Lord.*

These works, nearly a half million words, constituted a
bulwark of orthodoxy, and the clergy, recognizing More as
their champion, thought to reward him. They collected a
great sum of money, which he refused, giving as his reason
that if he were in their pay, he would no longer be a dis-
interested and unbiased defender. Some of his friends
pointed out that he was now a poor man and that it would
be well for him to accept so that his wife and children would
profit. But he was obdurate. When they offered him the
purse he said: "I had liefer see it all cast into the Thames,
than I, or any of mine, should have thereof the worth of

one penny. For though your offer, my Lords, be indeed very friendly and honourable, yet set I so much by my pleasure and so little by my profit, that I would not, in good faith, for so much, and much more too, have lost the rest of so many nights sleep that was spent upon the same. And yet wish would I, for all that, upon condition that all heresies were suppressed, that all my books were burned and my labour utterly lost."[6]

Death was in his mind and he made ready for it. He selected a marble slab and had a tomb prepared at the Church in Chelsea. He wrote his epitaph, stressing those things of which he was proud, and saying that, save for thieves, murderers and heretics, he had given no trouble to any man. He asked for the kind thoughts of those who would read the epitaph. "And that this tomb, made for him in his life time be not in vain, nor that he fear death coming upon him, but that he may willingly for the desire of Christ, die, and find death not utterly death to him, but the gate of a wealthier life, help him, (I beseech you good reader,) now with your prayers while he liveth, and when he is dead also."[7]

He had never forgotten his first wife, and to the tomb he had her remains brought. She who had given birth to his children was always "Dear Jane," nor did he ever cease to appreciate the virtues of the good lady who had brought these children up. "Oh how well could we three have lived," he wrote, "joined together in matrimony if fortune and religion would have suffered it. But I beseech our lord that this tomb and heaven may join us together. So death shall give us, that thing that life could not."[8]

Resigned to the future and confident that his course was

right, he sought to convey his strength to his family. "In the time somewhat before his trouble," recorded his son-in-law, "he would talk with his wife and children of the joys of heaven and the pains of hell, of the lives of holy martyrs, of their grievous martyrdoms, of their marvelous patience, and of their passions and deaths that they suffered rather than they would offend God; and what an happy and blessed thing it was, for the love of God to suffer loss of goods, imprisonment, loss of lands and life also. He would further say unto them that, upon his faith, if he might perceive his wife and children would encourage him to die in a good cause, it should so comfort him that, for very joy thereof, it would make him merrily run to death. He showed unto them afore what trouble might after fall unto him; wherewith and the like virtuous talk he had so long before his trouble encouraged them, that when he after fell into the trouble indeed, his trouble to them was a great deal the less . . ."[9]

In August of 1532 old William Warham, the Archbishop of Canterbury, died. Whom was Henry to nominate as his successor? With Anne Boleyn now openly living with him, and with the devious Cromwell in constant attendance, a choice was not long in forthcoming. It was Cranmer, he who had collected and arranged the opinions of the universities. But Cranmer was now in Germany observing Lutheran practices. And in the pursuit of his studies he had rejected his vows of celibacy and contracted a marriage with a niece of his host, a German clergyman. Nevertheless he was sent for, and leaving his bride, he returned to England. The formalities of sending his name to Rome were observed. The Papal Bull duly arrived, and Cranmer was made Archbishop and successor of Saint Augustine, openly following the ancient forms of consecration, privately wallowing in duplicity. Before the ceremony, he swore before witnesses, that no matter what he might say in public, his duty and his allegiance were pledged only to the King.

The plan was now advanced to its next stage. Parliament passed an act, giving Cranmer authority to settle the divorce. The clergy in Convocation agreed. The new Archbishop opened his Court at Dunstable. He first censured Catherine for her obstinacy in not appearing before him, and then, after a fortnight of mummery, he announced that the marriage of Henry and Catherine was no marriage at all.

While these events were happening, and supremely confident that they would happen, Henry had made Anne Marquess of Pembroke and, soon after, also had made her pregnant. On the twenty-fifth of January, 1535, he married her in secret. Not until the following Easter did he openly declare her Queen.

Preparations were made for Anne's Coronation. From her place of what was virtually imprisonment, Catherine sent an anguished appeal to the Spanish Ambassador: "I am separated from my Lord, and he has married another woman without obtaining a divorce: and this last act has been done while the suit is still pending, and in defiance of him who has the power of God upon earth. I cover these lines with my tears as I write. I confide in you as my friend. Help me to bear the cross of my tribulation. Write to the Emperor, bid him insist that judgment be pronounced. The next Parliament, I am told will decide if I and my daughter are to suffer martyrdom. I hope God will accept it as an act of merit by us, as we shall suffer for the sake of the truth."[10]

The Ambassador wrote to his master urging that the Emperor should send an army to invade England: "You cannot imagine the grief of all the people at this abominable government. They are so transported with indignation at what passes that they complain that your Majesty takes no steps in it; and I am told by many respectable people that they would be glad to see a fleet come hither in your name to raise the people . . . It is not to be thought that the King will be brought to the point by mild treatment, for his sin carries him away, and he is bewitched by this cursed woman in such a manner that he dares neither say nor do except as she commands him."[11]

But Charles had no stomach for war with England at this time. He was fighting the Turk both in Hungary and in the Mediterranean. He had his troubles with the Protestant Princes of Germany. There was unrest in Italy, and he was only too sure that if he made war with England, France would not be on his side.

The Coronation of Anne Boleyn was arranged with a lavish splendour that would have been worthy of Wolsey. There were great processions and tournaments and parades both in the streets and on the river. Flowers and banners and hanging embroideries, the clank of knights in shining armour, their gaily caparisoned steeds, guildsmen in full livery, apprentices on holiday, all combined to give the City a festive look. Bells were tolled, cannon were fired in long salute. Practically the entire peerage of the kingdom came to play their parts in the ceremony. But pomp and spectacle did not make the event popular. Noblemen and court officials might bend the knee to the new Queen, but as she, a shimmering vision of jewels and satin and velvet, passed through the streets, there were many heads left covered and there were cries of "Whore!"

Now that the divorce was an accomplished fact, it was thought that perhaps Thomas More, as a sensible man, would give up his passive resistance and attend the Coronation ceremony.

Two Bishops acted as the King's agents, but More declined the invitation, pleading poverty. Promptly they offered to pay for a velvet costume suitable to the ceremony. Again the ex-Lord Chancellor refused. In doing so, he recited a little tale. Once upon a time, it seemed, there was an Emperor who had condemned a maiden to die for some infringement of the law. But the death penalty could not be enforced because she was a virgin and he had previously decreed that no virgin should ever be put to death. His problem was solved by one of his council who said: "Why make you so much ado, my Lords, about so small a matter? Let her first be deflowered, and then after may she be devoured."

"Now, my Lords," said Thomas More to the King's messengers, "it lieth not in my power that they may devour me; but God being my good lord, I will provide that they shall never deflower me."[12]

He knew his Tacitus and was comparing the regime of the Emperor Tiberius with that of Henry. The Bishops were dismissed with a smile, but it is certain that the news they carried back to court was not received in a like manner. Anne Boleyn, at this supreme moment of her triumph, about to be formally made Queen of the realm, and with the heir of the realm, she believed, stirring in her belly, was affronted and angry. It was inevitable that Sir Thomas More would soon feel the weight of the King's displeasure.

The campaign to discredit and ruin him began with charges that he had accepted bribes when he was Lord Chancellor. More, brought before the Privy Council, to the surprise of everybody, readily admitted to having received a gilt cup as a New Year's present from the wife of an interested party. His admission brought great joy to Anne Boleyn's father, the Earl of Wiltshire. "Lo! did I not tell you, my Lords," he cried, "that you would find this matter true?"

More calmly begged the Lords to hear his part of the tale. After having drunk to her of wine with which his butler had filled the cup, and when she too had pledged, he restored it to her to give to her husband as a New Year's gift.

The next accusation again concerned a gilt cup. This time it was proved that More had accepted a cup from one by the name of Gresham, but it was also proved that he had given the donor a cup of far greater value in exchange. The next charge alleged that he had favoured a Mrs. Croker in his Court and that she had rewarded him with a pair of gloves in which were packed gold pieces. Quite readily More admitted that he had taken the gloves, but it was quickly shown that he had given the gold back to the woman with the words: "Mistress, since it were against good manners to forsake a gentlewoman's New Year's gift, I am content to take your gloves, but as for your money, I utterly refuse."[13]

More had taken his position and was resolved to maintain

it, but he was also determined that he would not be fool-hardy. Possessed of one of the best legal minds of England, he set about to employ his talents as though engaged in some ordinary business of litigation. The King's Council published a book of nine articles upholding the marriage. It was said that More had written an attack on this book and had plans to have it printed. Promptly he wrote to Cromwell: "I will, by the grace of Almighty God, as long as it shall please him to lend me life in this world . . . truly say my mind and discharge my conscience, as becometh a poor honest true man, wheresoever I shall be by his grace commanded. Yet, surely, if it should happen any book to come abroad in the name of his grace or his honourable council, if that book to me seemed such as myself would not have given mine own advice to the making, yet I know my bounden duty, to bear more honour to my prince, and more reverence to his honourable council, than that it could become me for many causes, to make an answer unto such a book, or to council and advise any man else to do it."[14]

Well aware of More's ability and eloquence, and also deeply conscious of his popularity, Cromwell, who was planning the attack, had no wish to put the former Lord Chancellor before an ordinary Court of Law. But there came, so he thought, an opportunity to trap More. The activities of a certain Benedictine nun were, at this time, attracting considerable attention. Her name was Elizabeth Barton, and she claimed she had seen visions and had been given revelations. The stories were credible enough to win for her a pious reputation, and to be called the Holy Maid of Kent. Many distinguished divines, including the Arch-bishop Warham and Fisher, were impressed by her and had gone to listen to her testimony. With his keen interest in all things pertaining to religion, More also visited and talked with her, thus giving Cranmer his chance. For the Holy Maid, in her supernatural venturings, claiming that she was speaking with the authority of the voice of heaven, had censured the King and declared that Catherine was his legal wife. She prophesied that Henry would lose his throne if he persisted in his alliance with Anne Boleyn.

Her statements could not go unnoticed. She had many followers including two priests, the Fathers Risby and Rich. Along with these two and some others, she was arrested, charged with high treason and finally executed. The names of Fisher and More were brought into the proceedings, and they were accused of being sympathetic to the woman and of neglecting their duty in not reporting her treasonable statement. Fisher had been indiscreet enough to listen to the nun's criticism of Henry's conduct, but with More it was different. He asked that he be given a public hearing, but his request was denied. Instead he was brought before a committee which consisted of his successor in office, Lord Audley, the new Archbishop of Canterbury, Cranmer, the Duke of Norfolk, and Cromwell himself.

In preparation for the tactics and strategies that he knew would be employed to ensnare him, More already had written a full account for both Cromwell and the King of his dealings with the nun. He admitted to having visited her. But when Father Risby had sought to tell him of her thoughts on the divorce, More had refused to listen, and when her other priestly supporter endeavoured to engage in a similar conversation, he had received like treatment. In fact, More stated, he had warned the lady in a letter.

"It sufficeth me, Good Madam," he had written, "to put you in remembrance of such things as I nothing doubt your wisdom and the Spirit of God shall keep you from talking with any persons, specially with lay persons, of any such manner things as pertain to Prince's affairs, or the state of the realm, but only to commune and talk with any person, high and low, of such manner things as may to the soul be profitable for you to show and for them to know."[15]

His statement had been received by the King and by Cromwell. Nevertheless he was brought before the special committee. At first, they treated him with elaborate kindness. Instead of dwelling on his alleged offense, they reminded him of the favours that the King had shown him in the past, and hinted that further rewards would proceed from the same source, if he were but amenable. Why, they asked, should he persist in obstinacy and go against that which had received the approval and sanction of both Houses of Parliament and the principal universities of Christendom? If he would but join in this approval, there was neither worldly honour nor profit that His Majesty would deny him.

More admitted the kindnesses that had been shown him by the King, but replied that: "I verily hoped that I should never have heard of this matter more, considering that I have from time to time, always from the beginning, so plainly and truly declared my mind unto his grace, which his highness to me ever seemed, like a most gracious prince, very well to accept, never minding, as he said to molest me more therewith . . ."[16]

The Council now changed its tactics. The mock solicitude was replaced by severity. If he did not fall in with their thinking, the King would believe "that never was there servant to his sovereign so villainous nor subject to his prince so traitorous as he." He was told that the King now regretted having written the *Assertion of the Seven Sacraments* and that as he looked back he believed it was More who had induced him to take up the literary cudgels on behalf of Papal authority.

This revelation of the King's thinking, and the promise of his anger, did not intimidate More. "My lords," he answered them, "these terrors be arguments for children and not for me. But to answer that wherewith you chiefly burden me, I believe the king's highness, of his honor, will never lay that to my charge . . ." He recalled the conversation in which he had advised the King to touch more slenderly on the Pope's authority, and Henry's acknowledgement that he was so bound to the See of Rome that he could not do it too much honour. "So that I trust," concluded More, "when his grace shall be once truly informed of this, and call to his gracious remembrance my doing in that behalf, his highness will never speak of it more, but clear me thoroughly therein himself."

After the delivery of this response, he was dismissed with a coldness that boded ill. He knew the King would soon learn of his stand, and he knew too that there could be no uncertainty as to his fate. But he had served his duty and his conscience, and the knowledge of this gave him such inner content that his son-in-law, who was anxiously waiting for him, misunderstood his calmness.

"I trust, Sir, that all is well," he greeted More, "because that you be so merry."

"It is so, indeed, son Roper," answered More.

"Are you then put out of the parliament bill?"

"By my troth, son Roper," said More with a smile, "I never remembered it."

"Never remembered it, Sir," said the startled young man. "A case that toucheth yourself so near, and us all for your sake. I am sorry to hear it; for I verily trusted, when I saw you so merry, that all had been well."

"Wilt thou know, son Roper, why I was so merry?"

"That would I gladly, Sir," was the answer.

"In good faith I rejoiced, Son, that I had given the devil a foul fall that with those Lords I had gone so far as without great shame I could never go back again."

And Roper records that upon hearing these words he waxed "very sad for though himself liked it well, yet liked it me but a little."

More conducted his case so correctly that for the moment Henry's purpose was delayed. The Council, in fear of public opinion, told the King, "for in this case of the nun he was accounted . . . so innocent and clear, that for his dealing therein men reckoned him far worthier of praise than reproof."[17]

When he heard this report, Henry exhibited a tremendous anger, and swore that he would appear before the Lords in person and by his presence insure that More's name would be included in the Bill of Attainder. His advisers dissuaded him from this violent action and convinced him that a better and more fit occasion would soon be found to punish More.

It was his daughter, Margaret, who told More that his name was not included in the Bill of Attainder which had been passed against the Holy Maid and her associates. She was happy in her information, but her father was wiser, telling her: "In faith, Meg, *quod differtur non aufertur.*" What is postponed is not abandoned.

The Duke of Norfolk was of this opinion also, and because of past associations, or perhaps conscious and apprehensive that any injustice or hurt rendered to a man so widely respected would result in a wave of protest and horror, solemnly warned him that the indignation of a Prince is death.

"By the Mass, Master More," he said, "it is perilous striving with Princes. And therefore, I would wish you somewhat to incline to the King's pleasure; for by God body, master More, *Indignatio principis mors est.*"

"Is that all, my Lord," was the calm response, "then in good faith is there no more difference between your grace and me, but that I shall die today and you tomorrow."[18]

He made another prophecy, this time to his daughter. She was telling him of the gaieties of the new Queen: "There is nothing else in the Court but dancing and sporting."

"Alas Meg, alas it pitieth me," he told her, "to remember unto what misery, poor soul, she will shortly come. These dances of hers will prove such dances that she will spurn our heads off like footballs; but it will not be long ere her head will dance the like dance."[19]

16

HE sought to prepare his family for the future. While sitting at dinner with them he would have a bogus official appear and, after a great noise at the door, go through the motions of arresting him. By the enactment and repetition of this little comedy he tried to get them used to the day that was sure to come. But although he professed a lightheartedness at the time, he, as he afterwards confided to his daughter, was often vexed with distress and anxiety. He told her of the many weary night hours that he had spent thinking "while my wife slept and thought I had slept too, what peril were possible to fall to me . . . And in devising, daughter, thereupon, I had a full, heavy heart."[1]

He had not long to wait. The day was rapidly approaching when Henry could fulfill his boast that he would be both King and Pope in England. In Rome on the twenty-third of March, 1534, it was announced that the marriage of Henry and Catherine was valid. A week later the English parliament passed an Act of Succession which made Anne Boleyn's issue the first in succession to the Crown and thus, by legislation, deliberately made a bastard of Catherine's daughter, the Princess Mary.

The dread charge of high treason would be the lot of anyone who would deny the new law, and a Commission was established to extract an oath of obedience from the Lords, both Spiritual and Temporal, and from anybody else who might be selected. The members of this Commission were the same men who had previously examined More, except for the Abbot of Westminster who took the place of the Duke of Norfolk. In administering the oath, they went beyond the bounds of legality; the statute which required all subjects to swear in the succession of Anne's children, now, thanks to a rider formulated by Cromwell and Audley, provided that those taking the oath should also acknowledge Henry as being the Head of the Church in England. And in doing so, they renounced all obedience to the Bishop of Rome, as having no more power than any other bishop.

The Lords and the Clergy were summoned to subscribe to the oath and, as the first layman of consequence, so was Sir Thomas More. It was on the Sunday following Easter, the twelfth of April, that he received the news. With Roper he had been to Mass at St. Paul's, and then the two had gone to visit his step-daughter and her husband, John Clement. It was on their premises that he was officially summoned to appear before the Royal Commission.

He went back to his own home and spent the evening hours with his family. It was ever his custom on what he thought to be important days to receive Holy Communion. The next morning he followed this procedure. Then came the sad and difficult moment of saying goodbye to his wife and children. He was journeying by water but he would not permit them to see him embark. He shut the garden gate himself. After boarding the boat he remained silent for a long time. The rasp and beat of oars provided a melancholy accompaniment to his thoughts. Presently his mood seemed to change for the better. Having met the issue squarely in his own mind, and made the fateful decision, he turned to the loyal Roper saying: "Son Roper, I thank our Lord the field is won." His son-in-law did not understand but, as he afterwards wrote: "Loth to seem ignorant I answered, 'Sir, I am thereof very glad.' "[2]

At Lambeth they said farewells and More was ushered in to face the Commissioners, Lord Audley, Archbishop Cranmer, the Abbot of Westminster, and Thomas Cromwell. Gravely he was told that it was his duty to prove his loyalty by taking the oath. He made no quick gesture of defiance, nor did he indulge in grand heroics. He was a lawyer, and in such proceedings he was on his own ground. He asked that he be allowed to study the Act of Succession. Permission could not very well be refused, and he was given the document. He read it carefully and said he was ready to swear to the Succession, for it had been made a law of the land by Parliament. But as for the rest, the acceptance of the King's Supremacy over the Church, he could not subscribe.

"I shewed unto them," he said, "that my purpose was not to put any fault either into the Act or any man that made it, or in any oath or any man that swore it, nor to condemn the conscience of any other man. But as for myself, in good faith my conscience so moved me in the matter, that though I would not deny to swear to the Succession, yet unto that oath that there was offered me, I could not swear without the jeoparding of my soul to perpetual damnation."[3]

They told him the names of the Bishops and Peers and Members of the Commons who had already taken the oath, but he replied that it made no difference to his thinking. The Commissioners were baffled, but before accepting his decision as being the final word, they ordered him to go into the garden and reflect for a few hours while they put the oath to others.

It was a clement day of an English spring and in the greenness of the garden, and under the serenity of the wide sky, there must have been torment in his mind as he pondered over the two courses that were offered to him. If he persisted in obeying his conscience, suffering would not only be his lot, but would be wreaked on his beloved family. Death would be certain but not necessarily quick. To enforce submission the rack could easily precede the scaffold. Before the final shadows came it was quite conceivable that there would be the long ordeal of torture. As he paced to and fro, he could observe the traffic of clergy who had come to subscribe to the oath. No problem appeared to disturb their minds. Most of them seemed cheerful and lighthearted enough, save for one exception, Nicholas Wilson. Like the ex-Lord Chancellor, this priest had been a friend of the King, in fact, he had been Henry's confessor, but he had refused to swear to the oath, and he was now being led to the Tower.

When More was brought again before the Commission,

he stated that his position was unchanged and his answer
was the same. They sought, by threat and every trick of
argument and cajolery, to sway him, but it was to no avail.
He would swear to the Act of Succession, but he would not
accept the King's authority in spiritual matters. The opinions of the Commissioners seemed to differ at this stage.
Cranmer, for one, thought that a compromise might suffice.

After much discussion, he was remanded to the custody
of the Abbot of Westminster. There he remained for four
days, and it seemed for a while that there might be hope
for him but "Queen Anne, by her importunate clamors, did
exasperate the King."

On the seventeenth of April, a Friday, Sir Thomas More
was ordered to the Tower. Richard Cromwell, a man who
had married Thomas Cromwell's niece, and who in doing
so had conveniently taken the name of her uncle, was
charged with delivering the person of the ex-Chancellor.
He noticed that More, out of respect for his former rank,
was still wearing the gold chain of office around his neck.
The younger Cromwell, like his uncle-in-law, was very
much the realist when it came to things made of the precious
metal, and realizing that the chain would be confiscated in
the Tower, he advised More to send it to his home before
they arrived at their destination.

"No, Sir," was the firm answer, "that I will not; for if I
were taken in the field by my enemies, I would they should
somewhat fare the better by me."[4]

They arrived at the Traitors' Gate, but the gloom of the
dreaded entrance to the Tower did not prevent More from
joking with the porter. In the same lighthearted vein, he told
an official who apologized for the wretchedness of the cell

he was to occupy: "Assure yourself, Master Lieutenant, I do not mislike my cheer; but whensoever I so do, then thrust me out of your doors."[5]

He who still wore a hair shirt and who once had thought of becoming a Carthusian monk was not going to complain of life in a cell. Nor was he to concern himself with worldly cares. In the beginning of his imprisonment he was allowed the amenities of pen and paper, and he wrote to his daughter: "Since I am come here without mine own dessert, I trust that God, by his goodness, will discharge me of my care, and, with his gracious help, supply my lack among you . . ."[6]

In an effort to explain why he had chosen imprisonment rather than swear to the oath, he not only stressed the illegality of the latter, but gave voice to his opinion of those who professed to advise the King. "I may tell thee, Meg, they that have committed me hither, for refusing of this Oath not agreeable with the Statute, are not by their own law able to justify my imprisonment. And surely, daughter, it is a great pity that any Christian Prince should by a flexible Council ready to follow his affections, and by a weak Clergy lacking grace constantly to stand to their learning, with flattery be so shamefully abused."[7]

It was difficult for his family to understand why he was so deliberately courting death. Even the one who was closest to his thinking, Margaret, tried to make him change his mind. He was forced to write her a letter in which once again he explained his position and then added, somewhat sadly, as her husband afterwards reported, that none of the terrible things that might happen to him touched him so near, or were so grievous to him "as to see you, my well beloved child, in such vehement piteous manner, labour to persuade unto me the thing wherein I have of pure necessity, for respect unto mine own soul, so often given you so precise answer before. Wherein as touching the points of your letter, I can make none answer. For I doubt not but you well remember, that the matters which move my conscience . . . I have sundry times showed you that I will disclose them to no man."[8]

If it was difficult for Margaret to understand; it was even more so for his wife, that good woman of direct speech and common sense. Having obtained permission to visit him, she came quickly to her opinion: "What, the good year, Master More, I marvel at you, that have been always hitherto taken for so wise a man, will now so play the fool to lie here in this close, filthy prison, and be content thus to be shut up thus among mice and rats, when you might be abroad at your liberty, and with the favour and good will both of the King and his Council, if you would but do as all the Bishops and best learned of this realm have done; and, seeing you have at Chelsea a right fair house, your library, your books, your gallery, your garden, your orchard, and all other necessaries so handsome about you, where you might, in the company of me, your wife, your children and household, be merry, I muse what a gods name you mean here still thus fondly to tarry."

More gave his answer with a smile: "I pray thee, good Mistress Alice, tell me one thing."

"What is it?"

"Is not this house as near Heaven as my own?"

"Tillie valle, Tillie valle!" was her impatient reply.[9]

But despite her exasperation, and the failure of her

reasoning, she continued to be the good, hard-working wife that she was, never desisting in her attempts to have him released and never ceasing in her attempts to try to make his incarceration more comfortable. At one time, when all his properties had been confiscated, she, in pathetic appeal to Cromwell, wrote that she had been compelled of very necessity to sell her apparel to provide fifteen shillings for "the board wages" of her poor husband and his servant, and begged him for the love of God to show his "more favourable help for the comforting of my poor husband and me in this our great heaviness, extreme age, and necessity."[10]

As the months passed the screws were tightened and his imprisonment was made more harsh. No longer was he allowed to take his afternoon walk outside his cell. The solace of a chaplain's visit was denied. Even pen and paper were taken from him, and for the remainder of his confinement he resorted to the scrawl of charcoal on whatever material he could find. Lack of writing materials forced him to cease work on his *Treatise of the Passion*. In this uncompleted work he dealt with the courage of martyrs and the inspiration they received from the saddest and most inspiring of dramas. "What though thou be fearful, sorry, and weary," he has the Christ say, "and standest in great dread of most painful torments . . . be of good comfort . . . for I myself have vanquished the whole world, and yet felt I far more fear, sorrow, weariness, and much more inward anguish too, when I considered my most bitter, painful Passion to press so fast upon me. He that is strong hearted may find a thousand glorious valiant martyrs whose example he may right joyfully follow. But thou now, O timorous and weak, silly sheep, think it sufficient for thee, only to walk after me, which am thy Shepherd and Governor, and so mistrust thyself and put thy trust in me . . . Take hold on the hem of my garment, therefore: From thence shalt thou receive such strength and relief to proceed . . ."[11]

The process of intimidation weakened a fellow prisoner, the priest Wilson, who had been committed to the Tower on the same day as More. In desperation he wrote to More asking if there were not some manner in which they could accept a compromise. More's reply was to the effect that he could only be the master of his own destiny and that each man should form his own opinion and follow his own conscience. The unhappy Wilson wrote back that he had decided to take the oath. Without the slightest hint of criticism, More told him: "I beseech Our Lord give you thereof good luck . . . leaving every other man to their own conscience, myself, with God's Grace will follow my own . . . whether I shall have finally the grace to do according to mine own conscience or not, hangeth in God's goodness, not in mine, to whom I beseech you heartily remember me in your devout prayers, and I shall and daily do, remember you in mine, such as they be."[12]

In spite of the stern conditions of his confinement, More managed to keep in communication with his daughter, Margaret. After the winter of 1534 we find him painstakingly scratching a letter with a piece of coal: "Mine own good daughter, our Lord be thanked, I am in good health of body and in good quiet of mind: and of worldly things I no more desire than I have. I beseech him make you all merry in the hope of Heaven. And such things as I somewhat longed to talk with you all concerning the world to come, our Lord put them into your minds, as I trust he doth, and better too by his Holy Spirit: who bless you and preserve you all. Written with a coal, by your tender loving father, who in his poor prayers forgetteth none of you all . . . And thus fare ye heartily well for lack of paper. Thomas More, Knight."[13]

Throughout his imprisonment Margaret was allowed to see him occasionally. This concession was arranged by Cromwell, who thought, perhaps, that the presence and sorrow of the favourite member of his family would bring about a change in More's thinking. She was permitted to be with him on the terrible day that Abbot Reynolds of the Monastery of Sion, and three of More's Carthusian friends, Houghton, Webster, and Lawrence, together with John Hale, Vicar of Isleworth, were executed. The doomed men were led by the window of More's cell. Father and daughter watched the procession.

"Lo, dost thou not see, Meg," he said, "that these blessed Fathers be now as cheerfully going to their deaths as bridegrooms to their marriage? Wherefore thereby mayest thou see, mine own good daughter, what a great difference there is between such as have in effect spent all their days in a strait, hard, penitential, and painful life religiously, and such as have in this world, like worldly wretches, as thy poor father hath done, consumed all their time in pleasure and ease licentiously. For God, considering their long and continued life in most sore and grievous penance, will no longer suffer them to remain here in this vale of Misery and iniquity, but speedily hence taketh them to the fruition of his everlasting Deity; whereas thy silly father, Meg, that like a most wicked caitiff hath passed forth the whole course of his most miserable life most sinfully, God, thinking him not worthy so soon to come to that eternal felicity, leaveth him yet still in the world, further to be plunged and turmoiled with misery."[14]

The monks were dragged to Tyburn, where a terrible death, in full and ferocious ceremony, was given them. Before a gaping mob which included the Duke of Norfolk, each man was hanged, then cut down before losing consciousness, his stomach ripped by the butcher's knife and his entrails exposed to his still seeing eyes. Houghton was the first to suffer the torture, and while being disemboweled he was heard to whisper: "Oh most merciful Jesus have mercy upon me in this hour." When he was dead, his head was hacked from his body, and the body itself, chopped into four pieces. His companions were forced to watch the frightful butchery, but they showed no fear, each in his turn marched to the gibbet, and each in his turn addressed the crowd as calmly as though he was delivering an ordinary sermon on an ordinary Sunday before an ordinary crowd.

Soon more monks were to die. No form of torture was spared to secure compliance with the implacable will of Henry. The Carthusians were particularly stubborn. Not long after the martyrdom of the first group, a second was examined before Cromwell. Upon their refusal to acknowledge the King's supremacy, they were imprisoned in the Tower of London; where they remained seventeen days, standing bolt upright, tied fast with iron collars to the posts of the prison, with great fetters bolted on their legs. They could neither lie nor sit, nor otherwise ease themselves, but stood upright, and in all that space they were not loosed for any natural necessity.

But it was Thomas More and John Fisher who were the

principal targets of Henry's ire and Cromwell's wiles. A few days before the second group of Carthusians were thrown into the Tower, the new Pope, Paul the Third, raised Fisher to the Cardinalate, thinking that by this gesture he might lessen, at least in some measure, Henry's cruelty. But he did not know his man. In savage jest, Henry declared that while he would not permit a Cardinal's hat to be brought to England, he would arrange for Fisher's head to be sent to Rome instead. "I will so provide," he said, "that if he wear it he shall bear it on his shoulders, nor any head shall he have to put it on."[15] An almost continual examination and questioning was now the lot of the two men, and both acted warily. They had refused to take the oath that the King was the Supreme Head of the Church in England, and for that they had been attainted and were now in the Tower. But, so far, they had not openly made a denial that the King was the Supreme Head, and this technicality was an important factor in the legalistic processes with which Henry surrounded his every barbarity. Every attempt was made to make them fall into the trap. Parliament had obediently made a law which declared it high treason "to maliciously wish, will or desire by words or writing or by craft imagine invent, practice or attempt any bodily harm to be done or committed to the King's most Royal person, the Queen' or their Heirs Apparent, or deprive them or any of them of their dignity, title, or name of their royal estates, or slanderously and maliciously publish and pronounce by expressed writing or words, that the King, Our Sovereign Lord, should be heretic, schismatic, tyrant, infidel, etc." Cromwell questioned More about the new law and demanded his opinion but he refused to discuss it. Audley then pointed out that

More's attitude was inciting others to follow his example.
More disclaimed the charge. "As touching the whole oath,
never withdrew any man from it, nor never advised any
o refuse it, nor never put nor will put any scruple in any
man's head, but leave every man to his own conscience,
and me thinketh in good faith that so were it good reason
that every man should leave me to mine."[16]

Richard Rich, the Solicitor General, and one of the most
dious and unscrupulous members of the unsavoury group
that were now so active in Henry's service, took an active
art in the examination. Professing sympathy, he came to
Fisher, infirm because of his age, terribly weak because of
his confinement. The Solicitor General spoke softly and in
onfidence. The King's conscience, he stated, was disturbed,
and Henry privately wanted to know for once and for all
his former tutor's true opinion. On the pledge of secrecy
the aged bishop sealed his own death warrant by stating
that he believed directly in his conscience, and knew by his
earning precisely, that the King was not nor could be by
the law of God Supreme Head of the Church of England.

On the seventeenth of June, Fisher was brought to trial
at Westminster Hall. He was accused of high treason in
that he had denied the King to be the Supreme Head of the
Church. He made no attempt to deny what he had told
Rich, but he pleaded that the fatal words had been extracted
from him under a vow of secrecy from the King. In his
defence he denied treason and stressed that his opinion had
been given privately to ease the King's conscience. He
appealed to "all equity, all justice, all worldly honesty, and
all civil humanity." But his words were as nothing. He was
pronounced guilty, and the usual and terrible sentence, that

he should be condemned to be hanged, drawn, and quar
tered, was given.

As it was a sentence that because of his ill health and
old age it was deemed impossible to execute, it was decided
that a simple beheading would suffice. Five days later, the
Lieutenant of the Tower came in the early morning to his
cell and informed him that it was the King's pleasure that
he should die some time before the forenoon.

"Well," said the bishop, "if this be your errand hither
it is no news unto me; I have looked daily for it, I pray you
what is it o'clock?"

"It is," replied the lieutenant, "about five."

"What time," asked Fisher, "must be mine hour to go
out hence?"

"About ten of the clock," said the Lieutenant.

"Well then," said Fisher, "I pray you let me sleep a
hour or twain. For I may say to you I slept not much this
night, not for fear of death, I tell you, but by reason of my
great sickness and weakness."

When the hour arrived he dressed carefully and went with
composure to the scaffold where, in the words of one who
was there, he was "a long lean, slender body, nothing in
manner but skin and bare bones, so that the most part that
there saw him, marvelled to see any man, bearing life, to
be so far consumed; for he seemed a lean carcass, the flesh
wasted away, and a very image of death, and as one might
say, Death in a man's shape, and using a man's voice."

As the executioner made ready, the old man was offered
a pardon if he would accede to the King's supremacy. He
shook his head and instead invited the prayers of those
who were waiting to see him die. He spoke bravely

"Hitherto . . ." he said, "I have not feared death, wherefore I desire you help me from fear and assist me with your prayers, that at the very point and instant of my death stroke, and in the very moment of death I then faint not in any point of the Catholic faith for any fear."[17] The frail neck was bared. The ax went high and another step in a man's sanctity was made.

It was the King's order that the headless body be stripped naked and thrown into a shallow grave. The head was placed on London Bridge.

17

FISHER had been tricked into denying the roya
supremacy, but it was not so easy with lawyer More
Different tactics, employed by different men, all act
ing under the command of Henry, were tried. To his cell
at various times, came the great men of the realm, each
with his own way of argument or persuasion; the presen
Lord Chancellor, Cromwell, the Dukes of Norfolk and
Suffolk, various members of the Privy Council. But alway
the response was the same. He had nothing to say save
"that the statute was like a two-edged sword: if he shoul
speak against it, he should procure the death of his body
and if he should consent unto it, he should procure th
death of his soul."[1]

Failure of others acted as a spur to the contemptibl
mind of the odious Rich. As an added harassment an

humiliation, it had been decided that More should not be allowed his pleasure of reading. Sir Richard Southwell and a Master Palmer were ordered to remove all books from his cell. Rich accompanied them, and while they were about their work he, adopting the sympathetic manner he had so successfully employed with Fisher, made conversation with More. He asked him: "Admit that there were, Sir, an Act of Parliament that all the realm should take me for King. Would not you, Master More, take me for King?"

"Yes, Sir," said Sir Thomas, "that would I."

"I put the case further," said Rich, happy in the belief that More was falling into his trap, "that there were an Act of Parliament that all the realm should take me for Pope, would not you then take me for Pope?"

"For answer," said Sir Thomas, "to your first case, the Parliament may meddle with the state of temporal princes, but to make answer to your other case . . . suppose the Parliament would make a law that God should not be God. Would you then, Mr. Rich, say that God were not God?"

"No," replied Rich, "that I would not; since no Parliament may make any such law."[2]

More would not carry the argument any further. The books were packed, and the men, having performed their duty, departed. The cell door was shut and the incident seemed ended. But it was not so, for in the evil brain of Master Rich the words of More were tumbling and revolving and becoming material for one of the grossest perjuries ever to stain the annals of English justice.

It was on the first day of July that the ex-Chancellor was taken to trial. He was made to walk on foot the distance from the Tower to Westminster Hall.[3] Nor was his route direct. It was decided that he should be displayed as an example of one who had fought the King's wishes. So, dressed in a rough gown, he was taken through the most populous streets. The results were different than intended, for his appearance served only to excite the pity of the people. The effects of his imprisonment and long ordeal were very evident. His shoulders were bowed, he was terribly thin, and his uncertain and faltering gait showed that he was not used to exercise. But although his body was near broken, his spirit was not, and so it was he arrived in the Great Hall where he had so often worn the golden chain of high office and wielded the highest authority in the land.

The indictment which was read to him was a voluminous document, but from the morass of words emerged four main charges: that he had given a malicious opinion on the King's marriage; that, while in the Tower, he had written to Fisher and had encouraged him to resist the supremacy; that he, himself, had refused to acknowledge the King's supremacy; that, in fact, he had denied the supremacy, and in doing so had also denied Henry his royal authority.

Sir Christopher Hale, the Attorney General, read the long indictment. When he concluded, the Lord Chancellor, Sir Thomas Audley, spoke: "You see now how grievously you have offended his majesty," he admonished the prisoner "yet he is so very merciful, that if you will lay aside your obstinacy, and change your opinion, we hope you may obtain pardon and favour in his sight."

"Most noble lords," was More's reply, "I have great reason to return thanks to your honours for this your great

CRANMER

civility, but I beseech Almighty God, that I may continue in the mind I am in, through his grace, unto death."[4]

The forms of a trial were to be followed, but there was not a man present—juryman, prosecutor, judge, the prisoner himself—who was in doubt of what the verdict and sentence would be.

More well knew his fate, but he was resolved to conduct his defence with every resource and knowledge of the law that was at his disposal. He voiced a fear that his memory and understanding, "which are both impaired, together with my bodily health, through a long indisposition contracted by my imprisonment, should now fail me so far as to make me incapable of making such ready answers in my defense, as otherwise I might have done."

These words and the very visible fact that he could not stand without leaning on a stick, induced the judges to allow him to sit while he spoke.

He began to discuss the indictment, and very soon his audience grew uneasy, for it was strikingly evident that here was a case of the mouse playing with the cats.

"As . . . to the King's second marriage," he said, "I confess, I always told his majesty my opinion, according to the dictates of my conscience, which I neither ever would, nor ought to have concealed: for which I am so far from thinking myself guilty of High Treason, that on the contrary, being required to give my opinion by so great a prince in an affair of so much importance, upon which the peace of the kingdom depended; I should have basely flattered him, and my own conscience, had not I spoke the truth as I thought: then indeed I might justly have been esteemed a most wicked subject, and a perfidious Traitor to God. If I have offended the king herein, if it can be an offence to tell one's mind freely when his sovereign puts the question to him; I suppose I have been sufficiently punished already . . ."[5]

The accusation that More had incited Fisher in various letters could not be substantiated by the Crown because the correspondence could not be produced. Fisher had destroyed his papers, but More told the court that he had remembered what he had written: "In one of them there was nothing in the world contained but certain familiar talk and recommendations, such as was seemly and agreeable to our long and old acquaintance. In the other was contained my answer that I made to the said bishop, demanding of me what thing I answered at my first examination in the Tower upon the said statute. Whereunto I answered nothing else but that I had informed and settled my conscience, and that he should inform and settle his. And other answer, upon the charge of my soul, made I none."

It was pointed out to him that Fisher, when being examined, had in one instance used phraseology similar to More's. If this were true, explained More, "that . . . happened by reason of the conformity of our wits, learning and study . . ."[6]

He readily admitted that he had declined to give his opinion concerning the supremacy, but he explained that he could not transgress any law or incur any crime or treason by holding his speech, God only being Judge of our secret thoughts.

This statement brought an interruption from Sir Christopher Hale, who said: "Though we have not one word or deed of yours to object against you, yet we have your silence, which is an evident sign of the malice of your heart."[7]

More was quick with a learned answer, quoting a maxim that was familiar in the practice of law: *"Qui tacet consentire videtur,"* he that holds his peace, seems to give his consent.

The great hall, packed with men of uneasy conscience, listened with attention as, in measured tones, More spoke of conscience and of the necessity for the liberty of silence:

"In things touching conscience, every true and good subject is more bound to have respect to his said conscience and to his soul than to any other thing in all the world beside; namely when his conscience is in such sort as mine is, that is to say, where the person giveth no occasion of slander, of tumult and sedition against his Prince, as it is with me; for I assure you that I have not hitherto to this hour disclosed and opened my conscience and mind to any person living in all the world."[8]

The trial was not at all proceeding according to plan, and sympathy for the prisoner was so manifest that Rich dropped his official role of Solicitor General and suddenly admitted himself as a witness for the Crown. He was sworn and he repeated the conversation that he had held with More in the Tower on the day when More's books were removed.

He told how, in answer to More's question, he had agreed that no Parliament could make a law that God should not be God. Then came his terrible perjury. More, he said, had deliberately answered that Parliament could not make the King the Supreme Head of the Church.

The lie was spoken. The perjurer abandoned his role of witness and resumed his part as Counsel for the Crown.

More addressed the Court. "If I were a man, my lords, that did not regard an oath, I needed not, as it is well known, at this time, and in this place, to stand here as an accused person." He paused for a moment, then turned and spoke directly to Rich.

"And if this oath of yours, Master Rich, be true, then I pray that I never see God in the face; which I would not say were it otherwise, to win the whole world."[9]

He gave his account of the conversation that had taken place in his cell, then once again he directly addressed the Solicitor General whom, as he pointed out, he had known and watched since adolescence: "In good faith, Master Rich, I am sorrier for your perjury than for my own peril. And you shall understand that neither I, nor any man else to my knowledge, ever took you to be a man of such credit as in any matter of importance I, or any other, would at any time vouchsafe to communicate with you. And I, as you know, of no small while have been acquainted with you and your manner of conversation, who have known you from your youth hitherto: for we long dwelt in one parish together; where as yourself can well tell (I am sorry you compel me so to say) you were esteemed very light of your tongue, a common liar, a great dicer, and of no commendable fame. And so in your house at the Temple where hath been your chief bringing up, were you likewise accounted. Can it therefore seem likely to your Honourable Lordships, that I would, in so weighty a case, so unadvisedly overshoot myself as to trust Master Rich (a man of me always reputed for one of so little trust, as your Lordships have heard) so

far above my Sovereign Lord the King, or any of his noble
counsellors, that I would unto him utter the secrets of my
conscience touching the King's supremacy, the special
point and only mark at my hands so long sought for; a
thing which I never did, nor never would, after the statute
thereof made, reveal either to the King's Highness himself,
or to any of his honourable Counsellors, as it is not unknown to your Honours, at sundry several times sent from
his graces own person unto the Tower to me for none other
purpose? Can this in your judgments, my Lords, seem
likely to be true?"[10]

It could not have been credible to any one there, and
the feeling for the prisoner was so evident that the alarmed
Rich, no doubt still smarting from the description of his
character, took the rash step of calling Sir Richard Southwell and Master Palmer to the stand, hoping that they
would be intimidated enough to become partners in his
perjury. Both men disappointed him. They were, they
stoutly swore, too busy packing books on that fateful day,
and had not heard the conversation.

Rich could not produce any other witness or further
proof. His statement was obvious and flagrant perjury, and
the case against More had collapsed. No one could harbour
the slightest doubt but that More was innocent of any of the
charges that had been preferred against him. But the implacable will of one man was stronger than any and all who
sat in Westminster Hall that day. Fear of Henry had dominated the entire proceedings, and the same apprehension
drove the jury, after deliberation of only fifteen minutes,
to deliver a verdict of guilty.

In unseemly haste to complete the sordid plan, Audley

began to pronounce the solemn words of judgment. But he was interrupted by More who calmly corrected him on a point of procedure.

"My Lord," he said coolly, "when I was toward the law, the manner in such a case was to ask the prisoner, before judgment, why judgment should not be given against him."

The embarrassed Lord Chancellor admitted the correction and More was allowed to speak. And speak he did with clarity and eloquence. The time had passed when he had need be silent.

"Seeing that I see," he answered, "ye are determined to condemn me (God knoweth how) I will now in discharge of my conscience speak my mind plainly and freely touching my indictment and your statute withal. And forasmuch as this indictment is grounded upon an Act of Parliament directly repugnant to the laws of God and his Holy Church, the supreme government of which, or of any part whereof, may no temporal prince presume by any law to take upon him, as rightly belonging to the See of Rome, a spiritual pre-eminence by the mouth of our Saviour himself, personally present upon earth, only to St. Peter and his Successors, bishops of the same See, by special prerogative granted; it is therefore in law, amongst Christian men, insufficient to charge any Christian man."[11]

The Lord Chancellor asked him if he deemed his opinion to stand better than the bishops, universities, and the best learned of the realm. He received the reply that, on the contrary, the majority of Christendom was of More's thinking.

"For I nothing doubt but that," he told Audley, "though not in this realm, yet in Christendom about, of these well-

learned bishops and virtuous men that are yet alive, they be
not the fewer part that are of my mind therein. But if I
should speak of those that are already dead, of whom many
be now holy saints in heaven, I am very sure it is the far
greater part of them that, all the while they lived, thought
in this case that way I think now; and therefore I am not
bounden, my Lord, to conform my conscience to the Council of one realm against the general Council of Christendom. For of the aforesaid holy bishops I have, for every
bishop of yours, above one hundred; and for one Council
or Parliament of yours (God knoweth what manner of one)
I have all the Councils made these thousand years. And
for this one Kingdom, I have all other Christian realms."

He pointed out that the Act of Supremacy was not only
contrary to the laws of Christendom but that it was also
counter to those of England. He spoke of Magna Charta
and he reminded the Court that the Act violated "the
sacred oath which the King's Highness himself and every
Christian Prince always with great solemnity received at
their Coronations."

The Duke of Norfolk spoke up, "We now plainly can
see that ye are maliciously bent."

"Nay, nay," replied More, "very and pure necessity for
the discharge of my conscience, enforceth me to speak so
much. Wherein I call an appeal to God whose only sight
pierceth into the very depths of a man's heart, to be my
witness. How be it, it is not for this Supremacy so much
that ye seek my blood, as for that I would not condescend
to the marriage."

At this point there must have been much discomfort in
the minds of the judges, for included in their number were

both Anne Boleyn's father and brother. The Lord Chancellor was disturbed enough to try and shift some of the responsibility of the condemnation. He turned to the Lord Chief Justice of England, Sir John FitzJames, and asked him whether the indictment was sufficient, or not.

The expected answer and support was given and now the terrible sentence was spoken. After being hanged and cut down, disemboweled and quartered, butchered pieces of his body were to be put on the four gates of the city, his head upon London Bridge.

Had he anything else to say?

"More have I not to say, my Lords," he told them, "but that like as the Blessed Apostle St. Paul, as we read in the Acts of the Apostles, was present and consented to the death of St. Stephen, and kept their clothes that stoned him to death, and yet be they now both twain holy saints in heaven, and shall continue there friends together forever, so I verily trust, and shall therefore heartily pray, that, though your Lordships have been on earth my Judges to my condemnation, we may hereafter in heaven merrily all meet together, to our everlasting salvation. And thus I desire Almighty God preserve and defend the King's Majesty and to send him good counsel."[12]

It was all over. The solemn procession formed to take Thomas More back to the Tower. The executioner's axe, with edge turned toward him, was carried before him. Sir William Kingston, who had witnessed the end of Wolsey, was in charge of the escort. Young John More managed to push himself past the guards, and kneeling at his father's feet, asked and received his blessing. Kingston, who had seen many severities, was so moved that he wept.

"Good Master Kingston," the prisoner gently told him, "trouble not yourself, but be of good cheer, for I will pray for you and my good lady, your wife, that we shall meet in heaven together, where we shall be merry forever and ever."

Not long after, Kingston confided to More's son-in-law that "I was ashamed of myself, that, at my departing from your father, I found my heart so feeble, and his so strong that he was fain to comfort me, which should rather have comforted him."[13]

At the Tower wharf members of his family and friends waited. Margaret, his favourite daughter, "without consideration or care of herself, passing through the midst of the throng and guard of men, who with bills and halberds compassed him around, there openly, in the sight of them all, embraced him, took him about the neck and kissed him, not able to say any word but, 'Oh my Father! Oh my Father!' "

He gave her his fatherly blessing, telling her that whatsoever he should suffer, though he were innocent, it was not without the will of God, and that therefore she must be patient for her loss. After separation she, "all ravaged with entire love of her dear father, suddenly turned back again, ran to him as before, took him about the neck, and divers times together most lovingly kissed him,"[14] a sight which made even the guards to weep and mourn.

Within his cell, More prepared for death with his usual philosophy. Was his end, in reality, to be more cruel than dying by sickness in bed? "Some we hear in their deathbed complain, that they feel sharp knives cut in two their heart strings. Some cry out and think they feel within the brain pan their head pricked even full of pins, and they that lie in a pleurisy think that every time they cough they feel a sharp sword swat them to the heart."

And supposing he did lose his head? To the greater glory of his soul's journey no man could come headless for "our head is Christ, and therefore to him must we be joined . . ."

Even in these last hours attempts were made to have him change his mind. But to no avail. He was told that because he had been Lord Chancellor, the more terrible part of his sentence was to be remitted. He was not to be hanged nor drawn nor quartered, merely beheaded. When given this information he wryly gave voice to the hope "that none of his friends might experience the like mercy from the King."

On the day before he was to die he took up his piece of coal and laboriously scratched his last letter to his daughter, telling her to convey his farewells and blessings to the various members of his family and a few friends. He gave instructions as to the disposal of a few belongings. "I cumber you, good Margaret, much, but I would be sorry if it should be any longer than tomorrow. For it is St. Thomas even* and the Utas of St. Peter†; and therefore tomorrow long I to go to God; it were a day very meet and convenient for me. I never liked your manner toward me better than when you kissed me last; for I love when daughterly love and dear charity hath no leisure to look to worldly courtesy. Farewell, my dear child, and pray for me,

---

* The eve of the feast of the Translation (of the relics) of St. Thomas of Canterbury, which was kept on July 7 in England, and observed throughout Christendom, though on another day. The feast is still kept in some English dioceses.

† Octave-day of the feast of Sts. Peter and Paul, June 29.

and I shall for you and all your friends, that we may merrily meet in heaven."[15]

With the letter, his final writing, he sent the instrument of penance, the hair shirt that she had so often washed, the secret that she had shared with him.

The next day was Tuesday, the sixth of July, 1535. In the early morning one of More's closest friends, Sir Thomas Pope, came to his cell. He had been commissioned by the King and the Council to inform More that he should die before nine o'clock.

Even at this moment More retained his composure. "For your good tiding I most heartily thank you," he said courteously. "I have been always much bounden to the King's Highness for the benefits and honours that he had still from time to time most bountifully heaped upon me; and yet more bound am I to his Grace for putting me into this place, where I have had convenient time and space to have had remembrance of my end. And, so help me God, most of all, Master Pope, am I bound to his Highness that it pleaseth him so shortly to rid me out of the miseries of this wretched world. And therefore will I not fail earnestly to pray for his Grace, both here and also in another world."

"The King's pleasure is further," he was informed, "that at your execution you shall not use many words."

"Master Pope," was the reply, "you do well to give me warning of his Grace's pleasure, for otherwise I had purposed at that time somewhat to have spoken, that of no matter wherewith his Grace, nor any other, should have had cause to be offended. Nevertheless, whatsoever I had intended, I am ready obediently to conform myself to his

Grace's commandments. And I beseech you, Good Master Pope, to be a meen unto his Highness that my daughter Margaret may be at my burial."

"The King is content already that your wife, children, and others of your friends shall have liberty to be present thereat."

More gave voice to his gratitude that such a consideration should be shown him, whereupon his friend broke down and, as the Lieutenant of the Tower had done the day before, he wept.

More tried to comfort him. "Quiet yourself, Master Pope, and be not discouraged, for I trust we shall yet see each other full merrily where we shall be sure to live and love together in joyful bliss eternally."

When this gentle admonition failed to stay his friend's tears, More utilized the wit that was so seldom from him. Then, as now, it was the fashion of men of medicine to hold in great importance and value the colour and content of a man's water. More picked up his urinal and gravely gazing into it, and employing the professional manner of doctor to patient said, "I see no danger but that this man may live longer if it please the King."[16]

The moment came when the cell door was swung open and Sir William escorted him from the Tower. He was dressed in a rough robe and he carried a red cross in his hand. His steps were uncertain but his spirit was strong. A woman pushed through the soldiery and offered him some wine. Legend has it that it was his step-daughter, Margaret Clement. He refused the wine saying that Christ at his passing drank no wine, but gall and vinegar.

There are always those who revel in the fall of the great.

A woman shouted to him, "You remember Master More, that when you were Chancellor you were my hard friend and did me great injury in giving wrong judgment against me?"

"Woman," was the answer, "I am now going to my death. I remember well the whole matter; if now I were to give sentence again, I assure thee I would not alter it. Thou hast no injury, so content thee, and trouble me not."

Another of the crowd, a man whom More had once saved from suicide, spoke through the halberds, "Master More, do you know me? I pray you for our Lord's sake help me. I am as ill-troubled as ever I was."

"Go thy way in peace and pray for me and I will not fail to pray for thee."

His weakened condition and the rude carpentry of the scaffold made his mounting difficult. He turned to Kingston and with a smile requested him to "see me safe up, and as for my coming down let me shift for myself."[17]

A vast mob had assembled to watch him die. They eagerly waited for his last speech for it was the custom to permit a man to speak freely before his last moments on earth. But it was not to be this time. The Sheriff intervened quickly, reminding him of the King's wish that his words were to be brief.

His words were brief but they were to be immortal. He asked the crowd to pray for him and to bear witness that he was dying "in and for the faith of the Holy Catholic Church." Then came the ever-to-be-remembered and glorious affirmation that he "died the King's good servant but God's first."[18]

He knelt and recited the noble words of the ancient

psalm, the *Miserere,* the Prayer of Repentance. *Miserere mei Deus, secundum magnam misericordiam tuam.* "Have mercy on me, O God, according to thy great mercy . . ."

Neither his humour nor his attention to the feelings of others deserted him during his last seconds. Noticing that the executioner seemed to be in distress he gave him the coin of gold saying, "Pluck up thy spirits man, and be not afraid to do thy office; my neck is very short; take heed, therefore, that thou strike not awry, for saving of thy honesty."[19]

They wished to cover his eyes with a piece of cloth but he insisted on performing the act himself. He put his head on the block and made his last pleasantry, telling the executioner not to strike till he had shifted his beard for that it "had never offended his Highness."

The executioner measured his distance. He did his work with precision. One clean blow and Thomas More's head was severed from his body. The King's will had triumphed.

The news of the execution was taken to him. He was playing at cards with Anne Boleyn. They looked at each other.

"You are the cause of this man's death," he said. Then leaving her abruptly he shut himself up in a closed room and was alone.

I. *Moreana*

THE first two biographies of Sir Thomas More were written during his lifetime. On July 23, 1519, Erasmus wrote the famous letter to Ulrich von Hutten describing More and his household, which was printed the same year. The second, an *Epitaph,* was written by Thomas More himself following his resignation from the Chancellorship.

Before the close of the sixteenth century there appeared four other important manuscript biographies. *The Lyfe of Sir Thomas Moore, Knighte,* by William Roper (edited by E. V. Hitchcock, Early English Text Society, 1935), was written some twenty years after the latest events recorded. Roper, the husband of Margaret, More's eldest daughter and favourite child, lived for sixteen years in the More household. It is a comparatively brief account comprising some seventy octavo pages which Roper passed among his friends in manuscript, and it was not until nearly a century after More's death that it was printed. R. W. Chambers refers to Roper's *Life* as "probably the most perfect little biography in the English language."

The first formal biography, *The Life and Death of Sir Thomas*

More, by Nicholas Harpsfield, a young friend of William Roper, was compiled from eight manuscripts during the reign of Mary Tudor. The greater portion of the material is extant elsewhere, but there are certain distinct contributions made by Harpsfield. The first edition, printed from a collation of the eight Harpsfield manuscripts, edited by E. V. Hitchcock and R. W. Chambers, was published by the Early English Text Society in 1935 (London, Oxford University Press).

A *Life of More* written by his nephew, William Rastell, was printed in 1557. This was an elaborate work comprising the "life and times" of More, only fragments of which have been preserved. Although the work is inaccurate as to dates and names, our loss is great, for Rastell was in a position to give an eye-witness account of many of the events in his uncle's life. These fragments are available in the Appendix to Harpsfield's *Life of More,* as is the *Paris News Letter,* containing an account of More's death.

Another important source is Thomas Stapleton's *Vita Thomae Mori* in *Tres Thomae* written in Latin and published in 1588. Stapleton was born in the same year and month in which Thomas More was beheaded, and his biography is based on verbatim accounts and family documents preserved by Dorothy Colly, Margaret More's maid, and the wife of John Harris, More's secretary. It was published in Latin in Douai, Paris, Cologne, Frankfort, Leipzig, and Graz, but it was not until 1928 that the first English translation, *The Life and Illustrious Martyrdom of Sir Thomas More,* by Mgr. Philip Hallett, was published in London.

Of the three composite English biographies in existence prior to Stapleton's *Life,* one was lost save for a single page preserved in the Bodleian Library. The second, *The Lyfe of Sir Thomas More, Sometymes Lord Chancellor of England,* written by Ro:Ba: about 1599, contains little that is new, being a careful compilation of the Roper-Harpsfield-Stapleton traditions. The third, *The Life of Sir Thomas More* (London, 1726), by Cresacre More, Thomas More's great-grandson, contains many small details not found elsewhere, but the author's unfortunate disposition to improve authentic sources vitiates the work and it must be used with care.

Of the more modern biographies, T. E. Bridgett's *Life and Writings of Blessed Thomas More,* published in 1891, ranks first. E. M. G. Routh's *Sir Thomas More and his Friends* (Oxford University Press, 1934) covers a much wider range of More's interests and activities than is implied in the title. R. W. Chambers' *Thomas More* (London, 1935) gives special emphasis to More's role as an English statesman, without minimizing his personal charm and martyrdom.

A letter sent to Dame Kathryn Manne by Dane John Bouge, Thomas More's personal confessor, which has been widely quoted for his reference to More's second marriage and his saintly life, appears in the *English Historical Review,* VII (1892), pp. 712-715.

Added to the above Moreana is a great wealth of biographical data which appears in Thomas More's own writings. The earliest edition, *The Workes of Sir Thomas More, wrytten in the Englysche tongue,* was published in London in 1557. A modern reproduction, *The English Works of Sir Thomas More,* in two volumes, edited by W. E. Campbell, with introductions and notes by A. W. Reed, R. W. Chambers, and W. A. G. Doyle Davidson, was published in 1931.

E. F. Rogers' *The Correspondence of Sir Thomas More* (Princeton University Press, 1947) not only furnishes a calendar for More's correspondence but affords ready access to much that is not available elsewhere.

The Book of Sir Thomas More, edited by W. W. Greg (The Malone Society Reprints) was published in 1911. It was the work of a group of Elizabethan dramatists, one of whom is thought to have been Shakespeare.

Utopia, the second part of which was written first, was published abroad under the editorship of Erasmus, More's friend, towards the end of 1516. More then revised it and sent it to John Frobenish at Basle to print. This edition bears the date of 1518. Meantime Thomas Lupset, a friend of Erasmus, brought out a reprint of the first edition at Paris, which appeared before March 1518. A fourth edition was printed in Vienna in 1519. All four of these editions were in Latin. No English edition was printed in England during More's life. The earliest English edition, translated by Ralph Robinson, appeared in England in 1551. The second edition was translated by Gilbert Burnet, and the third by Arthur Cayley. *Utopia* has also been translated into German, Dutch, Italian and Spanish.

II. *Social and Political Background of the Period*

Allen, P. S. and H. M., *Opus Epistolarum Des Erasmi Rotero-dami* (Oxford, 1908).

Burnet, Gilbert, *History of the Reformation of the Church of England . . . The Reign of Henry VIII,* edited by Nicholas Pocock (Oxford, 1865, 7 vols.), Vol. I.

Calendar of State Papers: England and Spain, edited by Bergen-roth and P. de Gayangos (London, 1866-1890), Vols. II-V, 1509-1525.

Calendar of State Papers Venetian, edited by R. Brown (London, 1869-1871), Vols. III-IV.

Letters and Papers, Foreign and Domestic, of the Reign of Henry VIII, Vols. I-IV, edited by J. S. Brewer; Vols. V-XXI, edited by J. Gairdner (1862-1910).

State Papers, published under authority of His Majesty's Commission, Vol I, King Henry VIII (London, J. Murray, 1830-1852).

Campbell, John, *Lives of the Lord Chancellors of England* (London, 1874), Vol. I.

Cavendish, George, *The Life of Cardinal Wolsey,* (Chiswick, 1825), Vol. I.

Farrow, John, *The Pageant of the Popes* (Sheed & Ward, New York, 1950).

Fisher, H. A. L., *The History of England from the Accession of Henry VII to the Death of Henry VIII, 1485-1547* (London, 1919).

Friedman, Paul, *Anne Boleyn;* a chapter in English History, 1527-1536 (London, 1884).

Foss, Edward, *The Judges of England* (9 vols., London, 1848-1864); Vol. V, 1485-1603 (London, 1857).

Hackett, Francis, *Henry the Eighth* (London, 1929).

Hall, Edward, *The Triumphant Reigne of Kyng Henry the VIII,* edited by Charles Whibley (London, 1904), Vol II.

Harleian Miscellany, edited by Thomas Park (12 vols., London, 1808-1811), Vol. III (1809).

Holdsworth, Sir William Searle, *A History of English Law* (12 vols., Boston, 1923-1938), Vol. V (1927).

Howell, T. B. and T. J., *A Complete Collection of State Trials* (33 vols., London, 1816-1826); Vol. I, 1163-1600 (1816). Contains accounts of the trials of Catherine of Aragon, Thomas More and Thomas Wolsey.

Lincoln's Inn, London, *The Records of the Honorable Society of Lincoln's Inn. The Black Books* (London, 1897-1902), Vol. I.

Lyte, H. C. Maxwell, *A History of the University of Oxford from the Earliest Times to the Year 1530* (London, 1886).

Marriot, John A. R., *Oxford, Its Place in National History* (1933).

Mattingly, Garrett, *Catherine of Aragon* (Boston, 1941).

Miscellaneous Writings of Henry the Eighth, edited by Francis Macnamara (1924).

Nichols, Francis Morgan, *The Epistles of Erasmus,* from his earliest letters to his fifty-third year, translated into English (London, 1901-1918), Vols. I-III.

Pastor, Ludwig, *The History of the Popes* (London, 1923-1953), Vols. VIII-IX (1923).

Pocock, Nicholas, *Records of the Reformation, The Divorce, 1527-1533* (Oxford, 1870), Vol. I.

Pollard, A. F., *Wolsey* (London, 1929).

Sergeant, Philip W., *The Life of Anne Boleyn* (New York, 1924).

Sullivan, Frank, and Padberg, Majie, *Moreana*, 1478-1945. A preliminary check list of material by and about Sir Thomas More (Kansas City, Mo., 1946).

NOTES

It will be apparent to anyone familiar with the material on the life of Thomas More that this book rests primarily on original sources. In matters of punctuation and capitalization, I have followed modern usage, preferring not to irritate my readers, and myself, by a pedantic usage which would add little or nothing to the validity of my story.

CHAPTER 1

1. Karl Kautsky, *Thomas More and his Utopia* (New York, 1927), p. 250.

CHAPTER 2

1. *The Poems of William Dunbar,* ed. by David Laing (Edinburgh, 1834), p. 277.
2. Nicholas Harpsfield, *The Life and Death of Sir Thomas More,* ed. by E. V. Hitchcock (London, 1932), p. 9.
3. *Utopia,* tr. by Ralph Robinson (London, 1869), pp. 36-37.
4. William Roper, *The Life of Sir Thomas More,* ed. by E. V. Hitchcock (London, 1935), p. 5.
5. Sir Thomas More, *Works* (London, 1557), p. 71.
6. Thomas Stapleton, *Life of Sir Thomas More* (London, 1928), p. 3.

7. Roper, p. 76.
8. *The Records of the Honourable Society of Lincoln's Inn, The Black Books* (London, 1897-1902), I, p. 703.
9. Richard Pace, *De Fructu* (Basle, 1517), p. 82.
10. Elizabeth F. Rogers, *The Correspondence of Sir Thomas More* (Princeton University Press, 1947), pp. 8-9.

CHAPTER 3

1. F. M. Nichols, *Epistles of Erasmus* (London, 1901), Vol. III, pp. 392-394, *passim*.
2. Translation by Archdeacon Wrangham, quoted by R. W. Chambers, *Thomas More* (Harcourt, Brace & Co., New York, 1935), p. 89.
3. Cresacre More, *The Life of Sir Thomas More* (London, 1726), pp. 29-30.

CHAPTER 4

1. Nichols, I., p. 389.
2. Allen, P. S. and H. M., *Opus Epistolarum Des Erasmi Roterodami* (Oxford, 1906), I, p. 6.
3. Nichols, III, pp. 387-399. Passim.

CHAPTER 5

1. Roper, p. 7.
2. Roper, p. 8.
3. John Campbell, *Lives of the Lord Chancellors* (Boston, 1874), II, p. 11.
4. October 21, 1515, from Bruges (see Rogers, *The Correspondence of Sir Thomas More*, p. 36).

5. To John Holt, c. November, 1501, Rogers, *The Correspondence of Sir Thomas More*, pp. 4-5.
6. Mountjoy to Erasmus, May 27 (1509), Nichols, I, pp. 457-458.
7. *Miscellaneous Writings of Henry the Eighth*, ed. by Francis Macnamara (1929), p. 175.
8. Nichols, I., pp. 457-458.
9. Ibid., II, p. 2.
10. *Works* (1557), p. 422.
11. Roper, p. 9.
12. T. E. Bridgett's *Life and Writings of Blessed Thomas More* (London, 1924), p. 130.
13. *English Historical Review*, VII (1892), p. 714.
14. Rogers, *The Correspondence of Sir Thomas More*, p. 78.
15. *English Historical Review*, VII (1892), pp. 714-715.

CHAPTER 6

1. Francis Hackett, *Henry the Eighth* (London and New York, Liveright, 1929), p. 109.
2. March 14, 1514, Nichols, II, pp. 121-122.
3. May 14, 1515, Nichols, II, p. 206.
4. May 4, 1516, Nichols, II, p. 260.
5. July 9, 1515. *Letters and Papers of the Reign of Henry VIII*, II, Part I, No. 679.
6. *Utopia*, pp. 28-29.
7. Ibid., pp. 33-34.
8. Ibid., p. 35.
9. Ibid., pp. 67-69, *passim*.
10. Ibid., p. 71.
11. *Works* (1557) *The Confutation*, Book II, pp. 422-423.
12. April 1, 1516, from Basle; Allen, II, p. 221; No. 396.

CHAPTER 7

1. Nichols, II, pp. 258-259.
2. Nichols, II, pp. 260-261.

3. *Venetian Calendar,* II, No. 691, February 24, 1516.
4. Nichols, II, p. 266.
5. Ibid., II, p. 169.
6. Thomas Stapleton, *Vita Thomae Mori,* V, p. 206.
7. Bridgett, pp. 92-93.
8. Chambers, p. 122.
9. Edward Hall, *The Lives of the Kings, Henry VIII,* Vol. I (London, 1904), p. 156.
10. Ibid., p. 157.
11. *The Book of Sir Thomas More* (The Malone Society Reprints, 1911), p. 76.
12. Harpsfield, p. 95.
13. Nichols, III, p. 2.
14. Ibid., p. 70.
15. Ibid., p. 103.

CHAPTER 8

1. Bridgett, pp. 130-131.
2. Stapleton, p. 72.
3. Nichols, III, p. 392.
4. Ibid., III, p. 361.
5. Stapleton, p. 77.
6. Harpsfield, pp. 23-24.
7. Roper, p. 11.
8. Ibid., p. 12.
9. See *Venetian Calendar*, II, No. 1072, 18 September, 1518.

CHAPTER 9

1. Roper, pp. 67-68.
2. Ibid., p. 68.
3. Papal Bull of Leo X, *Miscellaneous Writings of Henry the Eighth*, pp. 35-36.
4. July 24, 1521. *Letters and Papers of Henry VIII*, Vol. III, Part II, No. 1437.

5. Harpsfield, p. 87.
6. Ibid., p. 27.
7. Roper, p. 17.
8. Ibid., p. 19.
9. Ibid., pp. 15-16.
10. Ibid., p. 20.
11. Chambers, p. 211.
12. Roper, p. 21.
13. Dec. 18, 1526. Allen, VI, No. 1770; p. 443.

CHAPTER 10

1. Roper, pp. 24-25.
2. Rogers, *The Correspondence of Sir Thomas More*, p. 387.
3. A *Merry Jest, English Works* (1557), C.l.
4. *Supplication of Soules, English Works* (1557), p. 329.

CHAPTER 11

1. *Harleian Miscellany* (London, 1809), III, pp. 54-55.
2. Ibid., III, p. 57.
3. Ibid., III, p. 52.
4. Ibid., p. 53.
5. Ibid., p. 55.
6. Roper, pp. 32-33.
7. State Papers, Spanish, III, Part II, No. 224, 26 October, 1527.
8. Stapleton, p. 137.
9. Roper, pp. 36-37.
10. *Works* (1557), p. 1421.
11. *Works* (1557), p. 1419, 3 September, 1529.
12. Pastor, Ludwig, *Lives of the Popes* (40 Vols., London, 1923-
    1953), X, p. 3.
13. Ibid., X, p. 2.
14. *Letters and Papers of the Reign of Henry VIII*, IV, No. 4090.
15. *Harleian Miscellany*, III, p. 61.

CHAPTER 12

1. February 18, 1529, Campeggio to Salviati; see Ludwig Pastor, *History of the Popes*, X, p. 267.
2. George Cavendish, *Life of Cardinal Wolsey* (Chiswick, 1825), I, pp. 149-153.
3. Cavendish, I, pp. 157-158 and *passim*.
4. Ibid., p. 160.
5. Ibid., pp. 162-163.
6. Cavendish, I, p. 168.
7. Ibid., p. 176.
8. Ibid., p. 188.
9. Ibid., pp. 313-324, *passim*.

CHAPTER 13

1. October 25, 1529. *Letters and Papers*, IV, Part IV, No. 6026.
2. Hall, *Henry VIII*, II, pp. 164-165.
3. Roper, p. 51.
4. Ibid., pp. 41-42.
5. John Campbell, *Lives of the Lord Chancellors* (Boston, 1874), I, p. 40.
6. See Ibid., pp. 41-42.
7. Roper, p. 44-45.
8. Ibid., p. 45.
9. Stapleton, p. 63.

CHAPTER 14

1. Roper, pp. 56-57.
2. Campbell, *Lives of the Lord Chancellors* . . . pp. 46-47, *passim*.
3. Fisher, H. A. L., *The History of England from the Accession of Henry VII to the Death of Henry VIII*, 1485-1547 (London, Longmans, Green and Co., 1919), p. 308.
4. Hackett, *Henry VIII*, p. 299.
5. Hall, *Henry VIII*, II, p. 210.
6. May 13, 1532, *Letters and Papers*, V, No. 1013.